Celebrating Our Uniqueness

Daniel H. Gordis

Second Revised Edition

United Synagogue of Conservative Judaism
Department of Youth Activities

UNITED SYNAGOGUE OF CONSERVATIVE JUDAISM
DEPARTMENT OF YOUTH ACTIVITIES
Jules A. Gutin, *Acting Director*
Jacob Blumenthal, *Assistant Director*
Adam Feldman, *Program Director*
Ari Y. Goldberg, *Activities Director*
Jessica Steinberg, *Publications Coordinator*
Shalom Orzach, *Central Shaliach*
Yitzchak Jacobsen, *Director, Israel Office*
David Keren, *Nativ Director*

CENTRAL YOUTH COMMISSION
Marshall Baltuch, *Chairman*

UNITED SYNAGOGUE OF CONSERVATIVE JUDAISM
Alan Ades, *President*
Rabbi Jerome M. Epstein
Executive Vice-President and Chief Executive Officer

A publication of the National Youth Commission,
United Synagogue of Conservative Judaism,
155 Fifth Ave, New York, New York 10010
Second Revised Edition 1994

Manufactured in the United States of America
Cover design by Dirk Wunderlich

In memory of my grandparents

Meyer and Nehama Cohen

עטרת זקנים רב מזמות
ותפארתם יראת ה׳

(בן סירא כה:ו)

Acknowledgements

The invitation to serve as the author of this year's United Synagogue Youth Sourcebook was a great honor. I have learned a tremendous amount in the process of writing this book, and am very grateful for the opportunity to have been part of such a vital and vibrant element of the Conservative Movement's ongoing educational program. For the invitation to undertake this project, I am very grateful to Jules Gutin and Amy Wasser. Their enthusiasm about the project and their thoughtful discussion of the topic which the U.S.Y. staff had selected made this an exciting endeavor from the very outset.

Ever since the actual writing of this book began, I have received consistent support and assistance from the New York staff of U.S.Y. Jacob Blumenthal, Adam Feldman and Ari Goldberg each offered invaluable support; it is no exaggeration to say that this book could never have been completed without them. I also benefitted from the insightful and thoughtful critiques of a talented group of readers: Jacob Blumenthal, Rabbi Jerome Epstein, Adam Feldman, Ari Goldberg, Jonathan S. Greenberg, Esq., Jules Gutin, Rabbi Eliot Marrus, Steven Toltz, Amy Katz Wasser and Rabbi Joel Wasser. Each of them read several versions of each of the chapters, corrected significant errors, suggested improvements in style and substance and contributed to the development of the exercises and questions that follow each chapter. This book is vastly enriched for their many hours of work, and I am deeply appreciative to them as well. Of course, I alone am responsible for any remaining errors or deficiencies in the version now before you.

The writing of a Sourcebook such as this requires attention to a tremendous amount of detail. I was very fortunate to benefit from the talents of two University of Judaism students who served as Research Assistants in this project. Cherie Hershman, a student in the University of Judaism's Lee College, and Alisa Danon, a rabbinical student in our Ziegler School of Rabbinic Studies, devoted many hours to researching, proofreading, carefully entering Hebrew text and discussing the direction this volume would take. For their patience, diligence and warmth, my thanks.

I first began work on this project in the Summer of 1992, at which time I was serving as the Dean of the Brandeis Collegiate Institute at the Brandeis-Bardin Institute. One of my colleagues at BCI, a man who has become a trusted friend and valued teacher, is Rabbi Levi Lauer, Director of the Pardes Institute in Jerusalem. Much of this volume is deeply informed by the sensibilities and insights that Levi has shared with me over the years we have taught together. Though we had several very productive conversations regarding the basic outline of this project, Levi's imprint on this volume goes much further. He believes passionately in the importance of Jewish uniqueness and takes tremendous pride in that uniqueness, and I have been blessed to have spent these past several years teaching with him and learning from him.

It would not have been possible for me to complete this project in the midst of all of my responsibilities at the University of Judaism were it not for the Administrative Assistant in my office, Ms. Linda Watson. Linda's intelligence, loyalty and dedication are always instrumental in allowing those of us who work with her to successfully juggle more projects than we should ever think of undertaking. For her assistance with this project as well as with virtually everything else that I do, I am deeply grateful to her.

Dirk Wunderlich, the designer of this Book's cover, has been a pleasure to work with. I have worked indirectly with Dirk on a number of projects at the University of Judaism, and knew that he was the person to develop a concept that would be both visually appealing and appropriate to the topic. His artistic talent and hard work have done much to enhance this Sourcebook.

It would be impossible to adequately thank my parents, Dr. Leon and Hadassah Gordis, in this space for all that they have done throughout my life to enable me to work on projects such as this. Nonetheless, certain specific contributions they made to this volume should not go unmentioned. My parents were the first ones to point me to the volume on the Jaspers-Arendt correspondence discussed throughout these pages, and after all the readers and I had found what we were certain were all the mistakes in the volume, my parents read through a final draft and pointed to many important necessary corrections. For their assistance in this project, as well as in everything else that I do, my deepest thanks and love.

As is the case with any project of this nature, the last several months during which this Sourcebook was written have been extraordinarily hectic, to say the least. My wife, Beth, not only offered valuable ideas as this Sourcebook developed, but graciously stepped in to take care of our children when I really should have been with them. Our daughter, Talia, and son, Aviel, cannot wait for this project to be finished; I don't blame them, but hope that one day their own passion for Jewish life will help them understand why their father often seems to live at the computer.

I have dedicated my work on this project to the memory of my maternal grandparents, Meyer and Nehama Cohen. Though my grandfather died when I was a teenager, I still remember vividly his profound attachment and commitment to Jewish life. After he moved to Israel, he stamped each letter to us with a phrase that urged us to move to Israel so that both we and the Jewish State could flourish. I believe he would resonate to many ideas in this volume, but Chapter Ten is the one section which I am sure reflects his view of Jewish life. My grandmother, a teacher all her life, imbued all of her grandchildren with a love and respect for Jewish learning, and provided us a model of fierce and dignified pride in Jewish life and tradition. It is just over a year since she died, and I still miss her profoundly. In my own mind, there could be no greater tribute to her memory than the sight of hundreds of North American Jewish young people studying their tradition and grappling with some of its most difficult questions. That image is precisely what my grandparents lived their lives for. I miss them very much, and am deeply grateful for all that they taught me. יהי זכרם ברוך.

Daniel H. Gordis
University of Judaism
Los Angeles, CA

November, 1992
Ḥeshvan, 5753

Preface to the Second Edition

In the year that has passed since this Sourcebook was first written, I have been very gratified by the responses to it, and remain deeply grateful for the guidance, assistance and friendship of the professionals at U.S.Y. who made it possible. After a year of using the Sourcebook, we determined that a slight revision of the final chapter would make the material more useful to North American students. That chapter is essentially the only substantive change in this edition. I hope that the changes made here have been effective.

When I finished working on the first edition, I thanked my two children for their understanding of all the time this project had taken. Since that publication, our family has been enriched by the arrival of our third child, Micah Reuven. Micah is named for my paternal grandfather, Rabbi Robert Gordis. By far my greatest teacher, my grandfather was someone to whom the notion of Judaism as a sacred and holy venture meant a tremendous amount. I am saddened that Micah never got to meet him, but I pray that those values will be no less important to Micah than they were to the man for whom he is named.

Daniel H. Gordis
University of Judaism
Los Angeles, CA

August, 1993
Menachem Av, 5753

TABLE OF CONTENTS
תוכן העניינים

I.   **Introduction** 1

II. **Our Senses of Ourselves**

1.   Chapter One: עם סגלה 5
Am Segulah — The "Chosen" People?

2.   Chapter Two: עם קדוש 11
Am Kadosh — Holiness Through Separation

3.   Chapter Three: אשר קדשנו במצותיו 19
Who Has Sanctified Us Through Miẓvot

III. **Defining Ourselves in a Non-Jewish World**

1.   Chapter Four: כמשפחות האדמה 27
Jewish and Christian Images of "Law"

2.   Chapter Five: זכור ... אל תשכח 35
Jewish Tradition and the Value of Memory

3.   Chapter Six: אור לגוים 43
"A Light Unto the Nations"

IV. **Practical Explorations of our Uniqueness**

1.   Chapter Seven: אם אין אני לי מי לי 53
Our Obligation to Safeguard Jewish Interests

2.   Chapter Eight: כשאני לעצמי מה אני 61
Three Jews Who Faced Hillel's Dilemma

3.   Chapter Nine: ישנו עם אחד 69
Jewish Distinctiveness and Anti-semitism

4.   Chapter Ten: והביאותים אל אדמתם 77
Jewish Life in a Jewish Homeland

V.   Notes

    1.   End Notes 85

    2.   Works Cited 87

INTRODUCTION
הקדמה

Throughout our lives, many of us have heard the phrase "Chosen People" associated with both Jews and Judaism. Sometimes we may have heard these words used in a positive way; perhaps our grandparents, parents or teachers used this expression as they sought to encourage us to take our tradition seriously and to devote ourselves passionately to being Jews. But at other times, the cliché of the Jews as a "Chosen People" may well have had negative associations for us. Maybe we overheard someone arguing that when Jews call themselves a "Chosen People," it is a sign of arrogance or snobbery. Even if we have never heard anyone suggest that this phrase was inappropriate, we ourselves might have felt it. For many of us who have teachers, neighbors, relatives and friends who are not Jewish but whom we like and respect deeply, calling ourselves "Chosen" somehow seems unfair, unkind or simply wrong.

So, we ask ourselves, what does our tradition *really* say about this notion? Does our tradition really claim that we alone are God's chosen people? Why would God choose us? Does the claim that we are chosen amount to a claim that we are somehow *better*? If we do believe that being a Jew involves commitment to a special mission and to unique responsibilities, how do we express that mission and those responsibilities? How have Jews lived in the past to maintain their sense of uniqueness? Do we want to continue to sustain this sense of being "different"? What is important about feeling unique? Why is feeling "different" often so uncomfortable? Why do we also often sense that it is necessary? How should we live as Jews today in light of our answers to those questions?

This book was written in the hope that exploring the concepts of Chosenness, Uniqueness, Responsibility and related ideas will enable us not only to understand what our tradition has had to say about these issues in the past, but how we each feel about these questions today. The chapters in this book try to both teach us about some of the basic claims Judaism has made about uniqueness and to give us an opportunity to think about the roles these concepts play for us in the modern world. We will look not only at selections from texts such as the Torah, the various *midrashim* (rabbinic interpretations), the *siddur* (prayerbook) and other classic Jewish texts, but at modern books, personalities and incidents as well.

One of the interesting things we will discover as we work our way through these texts is that the idea that we are somehow chosen or unique is so deeply embedded in our tradition that it appears in numerous prayers that we recite on a regular basis, often without thinking about what it is that they mean. You may be surprised to see that important segments of the evening service, blessings recited for the Torah and Haftorah and *tefillot* like the Alenu make use of this concept. So if we are to open our Torah, our *siddur* or other crucial books in the Jewish tradition and feel comfortable with them, we will have to learn about Judaism and Chosenness; we will have to learn what it has meant, what it can mean, and how we feel about these ideas. The issues here are too important to Jewish tradition and Jewish life for us to ignore them.

You will see throughout these chapters that we pay a tremendous amount of attention to Jewish texts, and you may wonder why that is. Why is it that in each chapter, before we examine the role of an idea or a concept in modern Jewish life, we include traditional texts that have made use of that idea? It goes without saying that this collection of texts is not complete, and that our exploration of the themes surveyed in this book is only introductory. But even in this limited discussion of these issues, we focus largely on text. Why?

This book makes use of traditional sources because one of the central claims of Conservative Judaism has always been that a true understanding of modern Judaism can only arise out of an appreciation of Judaism's tradition. It is in our classic texts that each of us can begin to discover that tradition for ourselves. What is important for you to realize is that this book gives you the opportunity to read the texts of the tradition yourself, and to discover what *you* think it means and how *you* believe it should be applied to American Jewish life at the end of the twentieth century. The questions this book poses will ultimately have bearing on *your* life; you, therefore, should be the one to *read* the tradition and to begin to *think* about what it does and does not say.

For that reason, each of the texts here is presented in both the original Hebrew or Aramaic, as well as in an English translation. All of the translations are original to this book. Though there are many fine translations of these texts available, not all use the same style. Some translations seek to be more literal, and others more colloquial. This book translates all these passages anew. It presents these new translations so that students making use of them will understand them and find themselves able to discuss the ideas these texts suggest, and it also presents references to God in gender-free language. In that respect alone, these translations are somewhat less literal than many others. That is why we hope you will not study the translations alone. In addition to these translations, the original language is also presented, because when all is said and done, Hebrew is still the language of the Jewish people. It is the language of our homeland, the language of our prayer and the vocabulary of our Torah. So, try to spend some time on the Hebrew. You can always refer to the English, but remember that in the Hebrew, these texts take on a life of their own, and a sound and feel that make them uniquely ours.

As our discussion proceeds, you'll periodically notice the [☞] symbol in the text. That symbol indicates to you that some of the questions or exercises at the end of that chapter discuss a certain matter in more detail. Again, the purpose of these exercises is to make you an active partner of this process. We want *you* to wonder about the Jewish tradition, and to think deeply about what it means to *you* to be a Jew.

That, of course, is the point of this book. The entire Jewish tradition is yours, and, as we will see, it is designed to help us all become unique. How does Jewish tradition do that? Why is it important to be Jewish? How should our lives reflect our Jewishness? These are the fundamental questions we hope you'll think about as you work your way through the remainder of these pages. For too often, we expect people to be Jewish without their ever having thought about *why* that is important in the first place. This book suggests that there are important and wonderful reasons to be Jewish. We hope you enjoy the process of thinking about these questions, and that while you may reach preliminary answers now, the fundamental issues raised here will accompany you throughout your life.

Notes and Comments

CHAPTER ONE:
עם סגלה
AM SEGULAH — THE "CHOSEN" PEOPLE?

It would be difficult to imagine a phrase more commonly associated with the Jewish people than the words "the Chosen People." Indeed, the fact that both Jews and non-Jews use that expression makes it seem that those words must appear in the Torah, or if not in the Torah, in another classic Jewish text of major importance.

But, as surprising as it may seem, the words "Chosen People" do not actually appear in the Bible. A Hebrew translation of "Chosen People" would probably be עם הַנִּבְחַר (*am ha-nivḥar*), words which our Bible does not contain. Instead, the Torah speaks of us as עם סְגֻלָה (*am segulah*), or a "treasured nation." Is there a difference? What do these phrases really mean? In the next few pages, we'll examine some basic texts of the Jewish tradition, and try to learn exactly what it is that Jews have long believed about themselves. In order to begin to understand these issues, let's look at how the Torah and our *siddur* (prayerbook) describe us.

A Look at Some Original Sources

The original context of the phrase עם סְגֻלָה is from the book of *Shemot*, or Exodus. There, the Torah teaches as follows (Exodus 19:3-6): וּמֹשֶׁה עָלָה אֶל הָאֱלֹהִים וַיִּקְרָא אֵלָיו ה' מִן הָהָר לֵאמֹר כֹּה תֹאמַר לְבֵית יַעֲקֹב וְתַגֵּיד לִבְנֵי יִשְׂרָאֵל. אַתֶּם רְאִיתֶם אֲשֶׁר עָשִׂיתִי לְמִצְרָיִם וָאֶשָּׂא אֶתְכֶם עַל כַּנְפֵי נְשָׁרִים וָאָבִא אֶתְכֶם אֵלָי. וְעַתָּה אִם שָׁמוֹעַ תִּשְׁמְעוּ בְּקֹלִי וּשְׁמַרְתֶּם אֶת בְּרִיתִי וִהְיִיתֶם לִי סְגֻלָּה מִכָּל הָעַמִּים כִּי לִי כָּל הָאָרֶץ. וְאַתֶּם תִּהְיוּ לִי מַמְלֶכֶת כֹּהֲנִים וְגוֹי קָדוֹשׁ. אֵלֶּה הַדְּבָרִים אֲשֶׁר תְּדַבֵּר אֶל בְּנֵי יִשְׂרָאֵל; "And Moses went up to God, and the Lord called to him from the mountain saying: This is what you shall say to the house of Jacob, and tell to the children of Israel. 'You have seen what I did to the Egyptians, and how I carried you on the wings of eagles and brought you to Me. And now, if you listen to My voice and keep My covenant, you will be for Me *a treasured people* amongst all the people, for all the earth is Mine. And you will be for Me a kingdom of priests and a holy nation.' These are the words which you must speak to the children of Israel."

In this selection, therefore, God does *not* actually say that the Jews are the "Chosen People." Rather, says God, the Jews have the *opportunity* to become a treasured nation. The Israelites, later called Jews, become a treasured people, an עַם סְגֻלָה, not just by being born Jews, but by living in the particular way that God has chosen for us.

So, you might ask, is the idea of a "Chosen" people entirely the result of an incorrect or inexact translation? Does the verb בָּחַר (*baḥar*), which is Hebrew for "choose," really never get raised in traditional Jewish texts? As we will see, matters are not that simple. Although the Torah's most famous discussion of this issue, quoted above, does not use the verb בָּחַר, or "to choose," other important passages do. And it is probably largely as a result of these passages that the image of the Jews as a "Chosen" people has become so well known.

Several verses in the book of *Devarim*, or Deuteronomy, do speak of God actually choosing us. In Deuteronomy 7:6, for example, the Torah declares: כִּי בְּךָ בָּחַר ה' . . . לִהְיוֹת לוֹ לְעָם, or "for God has *chosen* you . . . to be a people for God." Many other verses also use this verb, but none of them are as well known to today's North American Jews as a few of the selections from the *siddur* that we recite often. But although we recite these prayers regularly, we rarely think about what they mean.

Think, for example, about the blessing we recite when we receive an *aliyah* to the Torah. As we come before one of the most sacred objects of all Jewish life, the Torah, what is it that we say? The blessing reads as follows: בָּרוּךְ אַתָּה ה' אֱלוֹקֵינוּ מֶלֶךְ הָעוֹלָם אֲשֶׁר בָּחַר בָּנוּ מִכָּל הָעַמִּים וְנָתַן לָנוּ אֶת תּוֹרָתוֹ. בָּרוּךְ אַתָּה ה' נוֹתֵן הַתּוֹרָה. or "Praised are You, Lord our God, ruler of the universe, who has chosen us from among all the people, and who gave us Your Torah. Praised are You, Lord, who gives us Torah."

Why would we say these words as we prepare to read from the Torah? Could it be because it is in the Torah that we learn what it is that God wants from us in order that we become the "treasured people" of which we spoke above? Perhaps our tradition seeks to remind us, as we prepare to read from the most sacred of Jewish texts, that when we read from the Torah, we are actually being told what it takes to *merit* being chosen by God. Maybe the point of the blessing is to remind us that being "Chosen," according to our understanding, does not mean being selected with no responsibility on our part, but being selected for a special role *if and only if* we live in such a way as to merit it.

A similar theme emerges as Jews welcome the Shabbat into their homes. As we gather around the Shabbat table and recite *kiddush*, we focus not on the significance or symbolism of the wine, or the beauty of Shabbat, but on what it means to be part of a special relationship with God. The words of the kiddush, which we know very well, try to remind us of that: בָּרוּךְ אַתָּה ה' אֱלוֹקֵינוּ מֶלֶךְ הָעוֹלָם אֲשֶׁר קִדְּשָׁנוּ בְּמִצְוֹתָיו וְרָצָה בָנוּ, וְשַׁבַּת קָדְשׁוֹ בְּאַהֲבָה וּבְרָצוֹן הִנְחִילָנוּ זִכָּרוֹן לְמַעֲשֵׂה בְרֵאשִׁית. כִּי הוּא יוֹם תְּחִלָּה לְמִקְרָאֵי קֹדֶשׁ זֵכֶר לִיצִיאַת מִצְרָיִם. כִּי בָנוּ בָחַרְתָּ וְאוֹתָנוּ קִדַּשְׁתָּ מִכָּל הָעַמִּים וְשַׁבַּת קָדְשְׁךָ בְּאַהֲבָה וּבְרָצוֹן הִנְחַלְתָּנוּ ... ;"Praised are You, Lord our God, ruler of the universe, who has sanctified us with Your commandments and who wanted us, and who gave us Your holy Shabbat willingly and with love, as a reminder of the Creation. For [the Shabbat] is first of our sacred days, recalling the exodus from Egypt. For You have chosen us, and sanctified us from among all the nations, and You have graciously given us Your sacred Shabbat." Once again, even as we gather to celebrate Shabbat, we begin by reminding ourselves that the Shabbat is (among many other things) a symbol of God's love for us, a gift God has given because we were chosen to be part of a special relationship with the Creator of the Universe. Chosen, perhaps, but not in the way that we usually think of that word.

So, are we chosen, or are we not chosen? The issue is not at all simple. What we have seen in this short review is that although the phrase "Chosen People" does not actually appear in the Torah, both the Torah and our *siddur do* describe us as chosen. Much of our tradition *does* claim that we have been chosen for a special role. However, does "chosen" mean "better?" [☞] Do Jews have a unique relationship with God only because we live our lives by following God's commandments, or because we are in some basic way preferable to other people? As we shall now see, equally important elements of Jewish tradition go to great lengths to suggest that all people of the earth are of equally great importance.

Many Jewish sources point to the Torah's claim that the entire universe is related, since we are all descended from Adam. [☞] If we are all descended from Adam, then all of humanity is in some sense family; we have a necessary connection to each other, and need each other.

The Talmud suggests (Sanhedrin 38a), for example, that even the way that Adam was created shows that he represents parts of all the earth: הָיָה רַבִּי מֵאִיר אוֹמֵר: אָדָם הָרִאשׁוֹן מִכָּל הָעוֹלָם כּוּלוֹ הוּצְבַּר עֲפָרוֹ, or "Rabbi Meir teaches: the dust from which Adam's body was created was gathered from all over the earth," and therefore, Adam represents all the people of the earth. In modern times, Jewish philosophers have made particular efforts to argue that being an עַם סְגֻלָה does not mean being "better." Let's look at a few examples of modern Jewish writers who have addressed this subject.

A Brief Look at Some Modern Opinions

Abraham Joshua Heschel, one of the great Jewish philosophers of this century, and a man who taught at the Jewish Theological Seminary for the majority of his career, wrote beautifully on almost every subject of Jewish life, and the question of the "chosen" people was no exception. Towards the conclusion of his *God in Search of Man*, he writes:[1]

> The Bible is a record of God's approach to His people. More statements are found in the Bible about God's love for Israel than about Israel's love for God.... We have not chosen God; He has chosen us. There is no concept of a chosen God but there is the idea of a chosen people. The idea of a chosen people does not suggest the preference for a people based upon a discrimination among a number of peoples. We do not say that we are a superior people. The "chosen people" means a people approached and chosen by God. The significance of this term is genuine in relation to God rather than in relation to other peoples. **It signifies not a quality inherent in the people but a relationship between the people and God.**

Professor Heschel makes the crucial point that there is nothing that Jews are *born* with that makes us chosen. Rather, the notion that we are a "Chosen People" is more a command than a description. It is a command that we live our lives with the sense that we are one half of a crucial partnership — a partnership with God.

Professor Steven Katz summarizes the tension in the concept of "chosen-ness" well, and makes the same point even more clearly:[2]

> By accepting the Torah, Israel became the "treasured people" of the Lord, a holy nation in the service of the Holy God. They entered into a covenant with [God], calling for unswerving obedience on their part and [protection] on the part of God. The election of Israel was not an act of divine favoritism. On the contrary,

it represented a mission involving special responsibility and corresponding retribution.

Professors Heschel and Katz both suggest that if we interpret the notion of "Chosen People" as implying that Jews are somehow better, wiser or more moral than other peoples, then we make a grave mistake. It is not that Jews are intrinsically better, they argue, but rather that Jews are invested in a unique relationship with God, and that as part of their unique relationship with God, Jews take upon themselves an obligation to live uniquely sanctified lives. When Jews speak of themselves as being "Chosen," we mean not "better" or "more deserving," but specially *obligated* to live in a special relationship with God. Nothing about this claim suggests that other peoples cannot have their own unique relationships with God as well. Indeed, the prophet Amos claims that the Philistines and Arameans had an Exodus just like that which God created for the Jews (Amos 9:7). When we say אֲשֶׁר בָּחַר בָּנוּ (*asher baḥar banu*), therefore, we really mean not "God who chose us," but God who has assigned to us a responsibility for unique living.

How do we achieve this unique way of life? As we saw at the beginning of this chapter, God tells the Jews that in order to be God's treasured people, the Jews must become a מַמְלֶכֶת כֹּהֲנִים וְגוֹי קָדוֹשׁ, or a "kingdom of priests and a holy nation." What does it mean to be holy? Do Jews have a unique way of seeking to become holy? As we will see, we do. In the next chapter, we will explore the meaning of the word קָדוֹשׁ (*kadosh*), and ask how, especially in this modern world, the Torah might want us to build holy lives in order that we might be worthy of being called "God's treasured nation."

Questions for Discussion

1. How do your non-Jewish friends feel about the "Chosen People" idea? Have you ever discussed it with them? Who brought it up? If you haven't discussed it with them, how do you think it would *feel* to have that conversation?

2. Have you ever felt that being a Jew involved you in a special relationship with God? What made you feel that? Was that a good feeling? Can you describe how you felt? Do you have that feeling as often as you would like?

3. Our tradition teaches that God made Adam the common ancestor for all human beings. But Adam was not, according to our tradition, the first Jew. That role was given to Abraham. What made Abraham different from Adam? What did he do? Can you think of actions in your own life which parallel the actions that Abraham took?

4. How can we fight the perception that "Chosen People" means "Better People?" If you could have your choice, would you say that Jews should give up the idea of "Chosen-ness" or should we hold on to it? Why?

Activities

1. Imagine that while in school, someone sitting at lunch with you remarks that for Jews to call themselves a "Chosen People" is "snobbish." What do you say?

2. Imagine for a moment that you are Abraham, and God suddenly speaks to you and commands you to leave your land, the place you were born and your family's city. God wants you to travel to a place that you know nothing about. What would you say? What would you want to know about being Jewish? How would you respond to God?

CHAPTER TWO:
עם קדוש
AM KADOSH — HOLINESS THROUGH SEPARATION

We saw in the previous chapter that God's promise to the Jewish people is not that we will be a Chosen People no matter how we choose to lead our lives, but that if we live according to the unique code of behavior that God has given us, we will be privileged to serve as a "kingdom of priests and a holy nation." We saw that in the very same passage, God refers to us as a "treasured nation" and then a "holy nation." What we did not discuss, however, is precisely *how* we go about becoming a "holy nation." In this chapter, we will look briefly at some of the most well-known sources which discuss precisely how the Jewish tradition suggests this transformation can take place. What we will see may surprise you!

Much of our tradition claims that one aspect of our holiness stems from our being separate from the other nations of this earth. This idea that we achieve holiness by being separate may make us feel uncomfortable. After all, you might well be able to recall instances in which you felt "different" or "excluded" because of your Jewishness; if you are like many other Jewish people, you may well have felt that this feeling was unfortunate, unnecessary. Is it *really* unavoidable that Jews will feel so different in a non-Jewish society? Can't we at least *hope* to live in a community in which we do not sense ourselves as the "other" — as those who don't belong or are very different. [☞] We will look at these questions in greater depth in other chapters, but for now, we want to explore the idea, perhaps strange or surprising, that our tradition sees at least part of this feeling of being "other" as necessary if we are to become God's "holy nation."

Two Rabbinic Sources on Holiness

As you might imagine, the rabbis discussed the concept of holiness at great length. The materials that they composed on this subject, called in Hebrew קְדוּשָׁה (*kedushah*), could fill more than a few volumes. But we will focus on two brief samples of their remarks.

The first text we will examine is based on the well-known verse in the book of *Va-Yikra*, or Leviticus. At the very beginning of פָּרָשַׁת קְדשִׁים (*Parashat Kedoshim*; notice the root קדש,

or holy, in that title), God issues a command to the Jewish people through Moses. In Leviticus 19:2, the Torah reads as follows: דַּבֵּר אֶל כָּל עֲדַת בְּנֵי יִשְׂרָאֵל וְאָמַרְתָּ אֲלֵהֶם קְדֹשִׁים תִּהְיוּ כִּי קָדוֹשׁ אֲנִי ה' אֱלֹקֵיכֶם, or "Speak to the entire congregation of the Children of Israel, and say to them, you shall be holy, for I, the Lord your God, am holy."

But what does it mean to be holy? How do we fulfill this *mitzvah*, this commandment? In the next chapter, we will look at the verses which follow this command and see what the Torah itself says about this issue. But now, let's look at what the rabbis said in the Sifra, an early rabbinic commentary on Leviticus. Speaking specifically about this verse, the rabbis wrote: קְדֹשִׁים תִּהְיוּ = פְּרוּשִׁים הֱיוּ, כִּי קָדוֹשׁ אֲנִי ה' אֱלֹקֵיכֶם; "You shall be holy means that you shall be separate, for I, the Lord your God, am holy/separate." What are the rabbis doing here? How do they arrive at this midrash, or teaching?

Their logic seems to go as follows. We are told to be holy, because God is holy. Now we have to ask a question that the midrash does not make explicit: what *is* the most obvious characteristic of God? And here the midrash offers an answer: it is God's separateness. The moment we begin to wonder about God, we discover that we cannot really know *anything* about God, because God is so separate from us. And *that*, says this midrash, is precisely the point. God's holiness stems largely from God's separateness; so, too, say the rabbis, *our* holiness should also derive from our separateness.

The Midrash we have just examined is one of the most commonly discussed *midrashim* in which the rabbis make the connection between holiness and separateness. But the same point emerges even more clearly in yet another rabbinic text which refers to the same verse. In Leviticus Rabbah 24:4, they write: אָמַר הקב"ה לְמֹשֶׁה לֵךְ אֱמוֹר לְיִשְׂרָאֵל, בָּנַי! כְּשֵׁם שֶׁאֲנִי פָּרוּשׁ כָּךְ תִּהְיוּ פְרוּשִׁם. כְּשֵׁם שֶׁאֲנִי קָדוֹשׁ כָּךְ תִּהְיוּ קְדוֹשִׁים, הָדָא הוּא דִכְתִיב "קְדֹשִׁים תִּהְיוּ"; "God said to Moses: Go and say to Israel, "My Children! Just as I am separate, so should you be separate; just as I am holy, so should you be holy." That is why it was written [in Leviticus 19:2] "You shall be holy." Here again, we see the tradition insisting that part of the process of becoming holy is becoming separate or distinct. This may not be the immediate association that we have with the concept of holiness, but it is a basic one in our tradition. [☞]

Other Traditional Links Between Holiness and Separateness

At this point, you might well be asking a question like the following. "Maybe there *are* certain elements of the rabbinic tradition that make a connection between holiness and separateness, but is that the view of the *entire* Jewish tradition? After all, why is it that I have not heard of this idea before?" This is a good question, but the truth is that many people who ask it *have*, in fact, heard of this before, without ever realizing that this is what they were being taught. Let's look at a few examples with which you may be familiar.

Think about one of the traditional Hebrew terms for marriage, קִידּוּשִׁין (*kiddushin*). Originally, the term *kiddushin* implied a legally binding engagement agreement, but for many centuries, since the ceremonies of engagement and actual marriage have been combined in Jewish life, Jews have often used the terms קִידּוּשִׁין and נִישּׂוּאִין (*nisu'in*; the more technically correct term for marriage) almost interchangeably. Think about that for a moment. Why would a word for engagement or marriage be based upon the root קדש, which we already know means holy? Does engagement or marriage make either partner in the relationship holy? Certainly not! But a traditional engagement in Jewish life separates the couple, so that each partner is set aside only for the another. The "holiness" of their relationship grew out of the fact that they were now "separate" from the rest of the community of unmarried (as well as married) people, and were "reserved" for each other. *That* is where holiness and marriage meet; marriage is holy when it separates two people off from the remainder of the community and has them pledge to devote themselves to each other. Here, as in Leviticus, separateness leads to holiness. [☞]

And just as we saw in Chapter One that parts of the *siddur* which we often recite reflect the concept of Jews as a Chosen People, it is also true that the *siddur* makes many references to separateness as an essential part of what it means to be a Jew. Remember the blessing that we say as part of the בִּרְכוֹת הַשַּׁחַר (*Birkhot Ha-Shaḥar*, or Preliminary Service) in the morning. One of the first blessings we recite reads: בָּרוּךְ אַתָּה ה' אֱלֹקֵינוּ מֶלֶךְ הָעוֹלָם שֶׁעָשַׂנִי יִשְׂרָאֵל, or "Praised are You, Lord our God, ruler of the Universe, who made me a Jew." Notice that just beneath the surface of this blessing lies another claim; if we thank God for having made us a Jew, we are also thanking God for not having made us non-Jewish. That, in fact, is how the original language of this blessing, still used in many traditional communities, appears in many prayerbooks even today. In many *siddurim*, the language you will find reads not שֶׁעָשַׂנִי יִשְׂרָאֵל, but בָּרוּךְ אַתָּה ה' אֱלֹקֵינוּ מֶלֶךְ הָעוֹלָם שֶׁלֹּא עָשַׂנִי גוֹי, or "Praised are You, Lord our God, who did not make me a non-Jew." Contrary to what many Jews believe, this blessing does not claim that Jews are better than non-Jews, or that there is something imperfect about being a non-Jewish person. All the language implies is that we are grateful to God for having included us in the unique relationship we began to describe in Chapter One, a relationship which demands our service to God through holiness, and therefore, through a degree of separateness.

As a last example, we turn to the Alenu, the prayer which appears at the conclusion of almost all services. We sing this prayer aloud often, though seldom aware that it makes the same point about our holiness and uniqueness stemming from a certain degree of separateness. So, let's look at its language once again.

The Alenu reads: עָלֵינוּ לְשַׁבֵּחַ לַאֲדוֹן הַכֹּל, לָתֵת גְּדֻלָּה לְיוֹצֵר בְּרֵאשִׁית. שֶׁלֹּא עָשָׂנוּ כְּגוֹיֵי הָאֲרָצוֹת, וְלֹא שָׂמָנוּ כְּמִשְׁפְּחוֹת הָאֲדָמָה. שֶׁלֹּא שָׂם חֶלְקֵנוּ כָּהֶם, וְגוֹרָלֵנוּ כְּכָל הֲמוֹנָם, or "It is our obligation to give praise to the owner of all things, to proclaim the greatness of the creator [of the world from its] very beginning, for not having made us like the nations of the world, and for not fashioning us as the [other] families of the earth. For God did not make our lot like theirs, and did not fashion our destiny like all of the multitudes." We conclude our prayer service by insisting that there is value in being uniquely Jewish. We suggest that had we become no different than the other nations of the world, the very essence of our being Jewish would have been lost, and something valuable — for us as well as for the entire world — would have been missing. [☞]

Separateness: Healthy or Problematic?

Our discussion of the concept of the Chosen People started out by demonstrating that the phrase עַם נִבְחָר does not appear in the Torah. Indeed, the Torah suggests that we will merit to be called God's Chosen People only if we live as God's "holy people" first. In this chapter, we asked how we are to become holy. What we have seen is that in our tradition, holiness is achieved by creating a certain degree of separateness. [☞]

But we also know that the Jewish tradition does not believe that we should be unconcerned about the world around us. Indeed, we'll see in upcoming sections that our tradition demands that we show concern for *all* our fellow human beings. How, then, can we accomplish both? How can we achieve separateness as part of our quest for holiness, and, at the same time be involved in and committed to the world around us? As we will see, this is not always an easy balance to achieve, but it is one that lies at the very core of traditional Jewish commitments. As we'll discover in Chapter Three, the crucial element in making this balance work is an appreciation of the concept of מִצְוָה, or "commandments" which are uniquely Jewish actions. That is the subject of our next discussion.

Questions for Discussion

1. This chapter has focused on the idea of Jewish holiness as stemming from "separateness." Can you think of examples when, in your own community, being Jewish made you feel separate, or apart? How did it happen? How did that make you feel about your Jewishness?

2. Think about the terms we've seen in the past few pages: holy, separate and unique. How would *you* define those ideas as they relate to being a Jew? Give some examples of how your definition relates to the lives of real Jews today.

3. Think about the community in which you live, or other modern communities which you know about. How would you complete this sentence: In my community, Jews are separate because . . . .

Activities

1. Put the idea of "separateness" on trial. Imagine that the idea of "separateness" is accused of hurting the cause of Jewish survival. What arguments would you make as the "prosecutor?" What responses or defenses would you offer as "defense counsel?" If you were on the jury, how would you ultimately vote?

2. This chapter mentions a metaphor that compares the marriage of a man and a woman to the relationship between God and the Jewish people. Make a list of the ways in which the two relationships are similar.

3. Deciding not to inter-date can often be difficult for many reasons. One reason is that we are afraid that our non-Jewish friends will think we believe we are "better" than they are. Now that you have studied the material in this chapter, try the following role play: have

one person be the non-Jewish friend who is insulted that the Jewish person will not date them, and have another person be the Jewish person committed to not inter-dating. See how the conversation progresses. For those people watching the "role play," how did each of the arguments make you feel?

4. You are the parent of a Junior High School student. You and your spouse are discussing where to send your child to school. Your spouse believes that public school would be fine, and that a Jewish day school would be too "separate." Do you agree? How do you respond?

Notes and Comments

CHAPTER THREE:
אשר קדשנו במצותיו
"WHO SANCTIFIED US THROUGH MIẒVOT ..."

The "Chosen People," we now understand, is a rather complicated idea. It does not mean that Jews are inherently better than non-Jews, or that we are "chosen" without any expectations as to how we should live. Being "chosen," or an עַם סְגֻלָה (*am segulah*), implies an obligation on our part to sanctify ourselves; we are expected to become a גּוֹי קָדֹשׁ (*goy kadosh*), or a "holy nation" (recall that we first saw this phrase in the passage from Exodus 19 in Chapter One). But becoming "holy," we have also learned, is not a simple matter either. Indeed, in Jewish life, holiness has the connotation of separation, of being "other," or different. That does not always feel comfortable, but it is an important part of how those Jewish communities which have survived have decided to live.

But these ideas, which we developed in the first two chapters, now raise a third question. Exactly *how* do we become different? Do we randomly select behaviors that no one else follows? Do we try to avoid contact with other groups and peoples entirely? Is it a Jewish ideal that we have nothing to do with our surroundings? As you might well imagine, and as we will discuss in detail later, nothing could be further from the truth! Not only is it acceptable for Jews to be part of the surrounding culture, we are actually *required* to share our values and ethics with other peoples. Often, we can learn, and actually *have* learned, from those around us. So how do we achieve this "holiness" and the "separation" it seems to require? Ironically, we actually answer that question ourselves each time we recite the familiar formula that begins many of our blessings . . . .

Miẓvot as the Key to Holiness

As Jews perform many of the actions which our tradition requires of us, we precede the action (or, in a very few cases, follow the action) by reciting the following words: בָּרוּךְ אַתָּה ה׳ אֱלֹקֵינוּ מֶלֶךְ הָעוֹלָם, אֲשֶׁר קִדְּשָׁנוּ בְּמִצְוֹתָיו, or "Praised are You, Lord our God, Ruler of the universe, who has sanctified us with God's commandments . . ." [☞] Each time we recite those words, we make explicit reference to what we believe it is that makes us holy: it is the commandments themselves. The mizvot, or commandments, serve this function in a variety of ways, of which we will mention only two.

In the previous chapter, we saw that part of the function of Jewish tradition is to make us holy through separateness. But holiness also has an additional connotation in Jewish life, that of purity. And the idea is reflected in the first of the two ways in which mizvot contribute to our becoming a גּוֹי קָדֹשׁ (goy kadosh). Our tradition claims that the mizvot have the effect of purifying us, or making us holy. The midrash in Vayikra Rabbah 13:3 claims that לֹא נִתְּנוּ הַמִּצְוֹת לְיִשְׂרָאֵל אֶלָּא לְצָרֵף בָּהֶן אֶת הַבְּרִיּוֹת, or "the mizvot were given to Israel only for the purpose of purifying humanity." Commandments might accomplish this goal in a variety of ways. First, the actual content of the commandment might lead to positive behavior. Thus, the commandment that we not speak ill of other people promotes a more loving and tolerant society. Similarly, the requirement of halakhah, or Jewish law (which is made up of the sum of the many commandments), that we treat animals with care produces people who act more kindly. The mizvah that traditional Jews pray regularly might well lead to human beings who are more introspective, who think about themselves and their role in the world more regularly than those people without opportunities for regular "spiritual exercise." And the list could go on . . . but what these few examples suggest is that one of the ways in which mizvot serve as the uniquely Jewish way to holiness is that they actually demand of us holy action.

But there remains yet a second way in which mizvot probably contribute to our becoming a גּוֹי קָדֹשׁ, or "holy nation." In this second function, the commandments bring Jews to holiness not only by requiring specific holy action, but by demanding discipline. The Jewish tradition claims that living a holy life committed to the improvement of our world demands constant effort. We all know that projects that demand consistent effort often become tiresome or frustrating. So our tradition has built into Jewish life a regular regimen of actions, called mizvot, to help us become used to the idea of disciplining ourselves. We are taught to pray regularly, whether we happen to feel like praying or not. Our tradition requires that we think about the foods we eat (and those we do *not* eat) whether we are in the mood to be spiritual or not. Whether or not we believe we need a day to wonder about the world and to taste a more perfect society, halakhah instructs us to observe Shabbat — whether we want to or not.

The purpose of this regularity is not to impose on us needless restrictions, or to make life unnecessarily difficult. The constancy of the miẓvot are the result of our tradition's belief that if we truly care about something, we will express that caring regularly. We would never imagine that we could love someone but fail to show that love regularly. And if we tried, we would learn that the love could not endure. And if we care deeply for a cause — the environment for example — it would not seem reasonable to us that we could make an impact by recycling only every other week. Either we care about something passionately and express that passion regularly, or our cause is not as important to us as we might have imagined it was. The same is true of our desire to become a "holy people," a people that seeks to reflect God's holiness in our own lives. Either we care enough to do this regularly, or we have to expect that we will not succeed. So our tradition gives us miẓvot, or commandments, with which to try to bring that holiness into our lives every day, with almost every passing action.

Of course, it is important to keep in mind that our tradition speaks of ideals. No one, regardless of how personally observant they might be, observes every commandment exactly as they feel they ought to. Each of us, our tradition understands, is on a path of moving towards the pattern of behavior we would like to adopt; that the tradition speaks of complete "regularity of observance" should not convince us that we should not even try because we will not be successful; rather, the point we ought to derive from this ideal is that *all* Jews have something to strive for. In that sense, all of us face the very same challenges. [☞]

As we have seen in the past, many of the important ideas in the Jewish tradition are expressed in the siddur, even in prayers with which we are familiar. And this concept of the regularity of miẓvot figures prominently in a passage we recite in ma'ariv (the evening service) called *Ahavat Olam*: אַהֲבַת עוֹלָם בֵּית יִשְׂרָאֵל עַמְּךָ אָהָבְתָּ. תּוֹרָה וּמִצְוֹת חֻקִּים וּמִשְׁפָּטִים אוֹתָנוּ לִמַּדְתָּ. עַל כֵּן ה' אֱלֹקֵנוּ בְּשָׁכְבֵנוּ וּבְקוּמֵנוּ נָשִׂיח בְּחֻקֶּיךָ וְנִשְׂמַח בְּדִבְרֵי תוֹרָתֶךָ וּבְמִצְוֹתֶיךָ לְעוֹלָם וָעֶד. כִּי הֵם חַיֵּינוּ וְאֹרֶךְ יָמֵינוּ וּבָהֶם נֶהְגֶּה יוֹמָם וָלָיְלָה; "You have loved Your people, the house of Israel, with everlasting love. [Therefore,] You have taught us the Torah, its commandments, statutes and laws. Therefore, O Lord our God, when we lie down and when we rise, we will discuss your laws and we will delight in the words of Your Torah and Your commandments forever."

This passage clearly reflects the importance of the regularity of miẓvot. It speaks of our commitment to observing our tradition's commandments "when we lie down" and "when we rise," and asserts that we will observe them "forever." Only with this regular practice and observance, the *siddur* seems to suggest here, can we feel the love that God has for us, and respond to that love appropriately.

Miẓvot as the Means to Separation

So far, we have mentioned two functions of the miẓvot. First, they require of us actions that make for a better world and bring out the "holiness" which lies in each of us. And second, because they demand consistency and commitment from us, they prepare us for the difficult task of living a life dedicated to reflecting God's holiness. But there is yet a third function that the miẓvot play in our path to holiness; the miẓvot also help us achieve the separateness we discussed in the previous chapter.

The Torah suggests that part of becoming the unique people described above is developing a unique way of living; the tradition suggests that to live as God's treasured people, Jews need to live differently from the other peoples of the world. That is yet a third function of the miẓvot. The Torah reading on Yom Kippur afternoon, taken from Leviticus 18, makes this point very clearly. Beginning with verse three of that chapter, God commands the Jewish people as follows: כְּמַעֲשֵׂה אֶרֶץ מִצְרַיִם אֲשֶׁר יְשַׁבְתֶּם בָּהּ לֹא תַעֲשׂוּ. וּכְמַעֲשֵׂה אֶרֶץ כְּנַעַן אֲשֶׁר אֲנִי מֵבִיא אֶתְכֶם שָׁמָּה לֹא תַעֲשׂוּ וּבְחֻקֹּתֵיהֶם לֹא תֵלֵכוּ. אֶת מִשְׁפָּטַי תַּעֲשׂוּ וְאֶת חֻקֹּתַי תִּשְׁמְרוּ לָלֶכֶת בָּהֶם, אֲנִי ה' אֱלֹקֵיכֶם, or "You shall not behave in the ways of the land of Egypt, in which you formerly lived. Nor shall you behave in the way of the land of Canaan, to which I am bringing you, and you shall not walk in their ways. You shall follow My judgments and obey My laws, for I am the Lord your God." Becoming God's treasured people, the Torah teaches, means behaving in a uniquely Jewish way. We are commanded not to live lives similar to those of the people from Egypt where we used to live, or similar to the lives of the people who live in our new homeland. Ours must be a pattern of behavior unique to us. *That* is the key to our holiness, and *that* is the function of the miẓvot.

Drawing Some First Conclusions

What have we learned from the material we have covered thus far? Essentially, we have seen a progression of the following three steps: (1) Jews are selected by God, according to the Torah, to be an עַם סְגֻלָּה, or a "treasured people." But that status as God's chosen does not come automatically; we have to earn it by living lives of holiness that reflect God's holiness. But that demand leads us to the question of "what does holiness actually mean?" That question leads us, in turn, to the second stage. (2) For Jews, a central element of the idea of holiness is the notion of separation. If we often feel different, or out of the mainstream, it may well be because that is *exactly* what our tradition wants of us, in order that we maintain our uniqueness. And how do we achieve this separation? That is the third stage. (3) For Jews, uniqueness is an important value. For traditional Jews, one of the key means of living unique lives is the decision to live lives committed to the observance of miẓvot. The miẓvot not only lead us to ethical behavior, they create for us patterns of living that are uniquely our own.

Very often, as we consider the impact that living a traditional Jewish life might have on us and our relationship to those around us, we realize that we will appear different and act very differently from some of our friends and neighbors. "Why would I ever choose that?" we wonder. If we think of wearing a *kippah* in public, we realize we will immediately be identified as Jews, wherever we go. Should we decide to observe Shabbat, there might be activities at school or with friends in which we cannot participate. When we consider kashrut, we understand it may well present at least some obstacles to eating with our friends. And often, we decide that for these reasons, we will not adopt these traditions and miẓvot.

But now we have added new questions to think about. Perhaps this separation is not an "accident" of traditional Jewish life, but part of its very purpose! Perhaps our tradition is reminding us of the expectation that we live lives of holiness, and of the Jewish perception that a key to holiness is separation. That may be a very new way of thinking for many of us, but it is certainly worth wondering about.

Before we move on to the next major section of this Sourcebook, we will devote one more chapter to the issue of miẓvot, and will examine the Christian attitude toward the idea of holiness achieved through commandments. Because as North Americans we live in a Christian community, we tend to see certain views as "natural" or "given," without realizing that they are distinctly Christian. Some of the difficulties that many of us have with the idea of achieving holiness through miẓvot stem from distinctly Christian ideas that we have taken upon ourselves. Our next chapter will look at some of those more closely.

Questions for Discussion

1. At times, the very thought of trying to fill our lives with the observance of miẓvot is complicated by our fear that if we're going to be honest about that commitment, it really should be "all or nothing." What are some ways in which you think you might *begin* the process of observing more Jewish traditions without feeling this way?

2. List as many blessings which contain the words אֲשֶׁר קִדְּשָׁנוּ בְּמִצְוֹתָיו (*asher kiddeshanu be-miẓvotav*) as you can. What type of behavior is associated with each of these blessings? Can you think of any characteristics which these behaviors have in common?

3. We've suggested that the phrase אֲשֶׁר קִדְּשָׁנוּ בְּמִצְוֹתָיו (*asher kiddeshanu be-miẓvotav*) is designed to remind us that the action which follows that blessing should sanctify us. Given that orientation, can you think of any human actions that you believe *should* have blessings associated with them, but do not? How would you go about finding out what the appropriate blessing for a certain action is?

Activities

In their discussions of prayer, our rabbis distinguished between two different ideals. One they called *kevah*, which means "fixed." They used that term to refer to the ideal of praying regularly, at fixed times, regardless of how we actually *felt* at the moment. The other term they employed was *kavvanah*, which means "intention." *That* term refers to the ideal of praying when we actually *feel* moved to pray. The rabbis understood this tension, but never resolved it.

Use this distinction between *kevah* and *kavvanah* to stage a debate about the whole idea of miẓvot. Should our actions be commanded, or should we perform these special rituals only when we feel particularly moved to do so? How would you explain the fact that the Talmud

suggests (in Bava Kamma 87a and elsewhere) that גָּדוֹל הַמְצוּוֶּה וְעוֹשֶׂה מִמִּי שֶׁאֵינוּ מְצוּוֶּה
וְעוֹשֶׂה; "the person who performs [commandments] because they are commanded is greater than the one who performs [commandments] without being commanded?" Try to critique that position. Have someone else defend it. Whose argument seems stronger to you? Why do you imagine our tradition makes this claim?

CHAPTER FOUR:
כמשפחות האדמה?
JEWISH AND CHRISTIAN IMAGES OF "LAW"

In the last three chapters, we have explored various elements of the Jewish tradition dealing with our uniqueness. While that is an important and appropriate place to begin, we ought not forget that the central theme of this Sourcebook is living Jewishly in a non-Jewish world. While we are interested in what our tradition has to say about us, we also want to know how what our tradition says affects our lives in a country which is mostly non-Jewish, and indeed, Christian.

There are a number of possible ways to explore the question of what it is like to live as a Jew in a non-Jewish world. One way would be to see what our tradition says about that. We will do that later in this Sourcebook, particularly in the chapter that deals with the concept of אוֹר לַגּוֹיִם, or the image of Jews as a "light unto the nations." However, looking at our own tradition is not the only way to think about Jewish life in a non-Jewish world. Another way is to examine the beliefs and claims of those people who live around us, for it is not possible for us to live in a non-Jewish culture without some of that culture's ideas coming to influence us very deeply, sometimes even without our realizing it.

Asking Some New Questions

How can we begin to discover the ways in which the culture we live in has influenced us? Let's ask the question in a different way. When we noted in Chapter Two that the "Alenu" reads: שֶׁלֹּא עָשָׂנוּ כְּגוֹיֵי הָאֲרָצוֹת, וְלֹא שָׂמָנוּ כְּמִשְׁפְּחוֹת הָאֲדָמָה and suggests that we owe thanks to God for "not having made us like the nations of the world, and for not fashioning us as the [other] families of the earth," how do we really know that is true? How can we tell if we really are unlike those who live around us? The answer is relatively simple. We need to learn a little about that culture itself. We will begin that process in the next two chapters. In this chapter, we will explore the Christian attitude toward commandment, or law, and compare that position to the Jewish viewpoint we have already discussed. In the next chapter, we will explore the different ways in which western culture and Jews make use of memory. In each case, we will attempt to ask ourselves to what degree the non-Jewish ideas and attitudes which surround us each and every day color our thinking, often in ways that are subtle and difficult to discern.

A Review of Judaism and "Law"

As you recall, Chapter Three explained that Judaism makes the essential claim that the way for Jews to achieve holiness and uniqueness is through the observance of Jewish law, or *halakhah*. [☞] Earlier in this Sourcebook, we quoted the selection from the Torah in which God commands the Jewish people to be holy. But when we did so, we quoted only the first part of the passage. To revisit the point of Chapter Three only briefly, let's examine that passage one more time, this time with the verses that follow it. As you may recall, in Leviticus (Va-Yikra) chapter 19, God tells the Jewish people: דַּבֵּר אֶל כָּל עֲדַת בְּנֵי יִשְׂרָאֵל וְאָמַרְתָּ אֲלֵהֶם קְדֹשִׁים תִּהְיוּ כִּי קָדוֹשׁ אֲנִי ה' אֱלֹקֵיכֶם, or "Speak to the entire congregation of the Children of Israel, and say to them, you shall be holy, for I, the Lord your God, am holy." Then the Torah continues immediately with the following: אֶל . . . אִישׁ אִמּוֹ וְאָבִיו תִּירָאוּ וְאֶת שַׁבְּתֹתַי תִּשְׁמֹרוּ. תִּפְנוּ אֶל הָאֱלִילִם וֵאלֹהֵי מַסֵּכָה לֹא תַעֲשׂוּ לָכֶם. . . לֹא תְקַלֵּל חֵרֵשׁ וְלִפְנֵי עִוֵּר לֹא תִתֵּן מִכְשֹׁל . . . לֹא תֵלֵךְ רָכִיל בְּעַמֶּיךָ, thus demanding that "Each one of you shall revere your mother and your father, and keep My Sabbaths. . . Do not turn to worship idols, and do not make for yourselves metal gods. . . Do not curse a deaf person, and place no stumbling block before the blind. . . Do not become a tale-bearer among your nation."

What does the Torah teach us as soon as God says קְדֹשִׁים תִּהְיוּ, or "You shall be holy?" God instructs us on how to accomplish that. Observance of the miẓvot is the key to our holiness, and all types of miẓvot are included. The Torah lists both those which regulate only our relationship with God (such as the commandment to observe Shabbat and the prohibition on making false gods) as well as those which deal with our relationships with other human beings (such as the treatment of deaf and blind people, treatment of our parents and the prohibition on tale-bearing). The Torah makes no suggestion that one category is more important than the other. Each is equally required if we are to seek to become holy; for Jews, the path to holiness (and therefore our uniqueness) is the observance of the law.

The Path to Holiness in Christianity

Since Christianity emerged from the Jewish community during the last years of the Second Temple period (the Temple was destroyed in 70 C.E.), one might expect that Jews and Christians would share a very similar approach to the importance of law as we seek to become holy and live up to God's expectations. But as we shall now see, that is not entirely the case. In fact, one of the most central areas of difference between Jews and Christians lies in precisely this area.

Let's look at one of the most important passages in the Christian Bible which deals with the role of law. Taken from Paul's Letter to the Romans, more commonly known as the book of Romans, it expresses relatively clearly early Christianity's approach to the role of law and commandment in human life.

Paul, or St. Paul as he is known to Christians, was an educated Jew, who died only a few years before the destruction of the second Temple. Thus, we know that he was thoroughly familiar with the account of holiness from Leviticus which we just cited. However, by the time he became a leading thinker in the movement which would later become Christianity, his views had changed dramatically. In Romans, trying to describe exactly how one achieves "salvation," or lives his life ideally, Paul explained that after the death of Jesus (also a Jew), something dramatic had changed in the way people should achieve holiness and seek a relationship with God:[3]

> 7:6 . . . Now we are rid of the Law, freed by [Jesus'] death from our imprisonment, free to serve in the new spiritual way and not the old way of a written law. 7:7 . . . What I mean is that I would not have known what sin was had it not been for the law. 7:8 If the [Torah] had not said [in the Ten Commandments] "You shall not covet," I would not have known what it means to covet. . . . when there is no law, sin is dead.

Notice how different this is from the Torah's viewpoint! The Torah suggests that observance of the commandments (or law, as Paul calls it) will lead to holiness; Paul believes, however, that law actually *causes* sin! This disparaging attitude to the law is reflected in numerous examples in many books of the Christian Bible; we'll refer to only two others, both of which are very well known. [☞]

In another example in Romans, Paul discusses circumcision, which the Jewish tradition requires of every male child at the age of eight days (unless some medical condition requires delaying the procedure). In a famous passage, Paul insists that what really matters is not whether a man is *physically* circumcised, but whether he reflects in his life the *attitudes* which circumcision addresses. Therefore, says Paul (in Romans 15:11):

> The real Jew is the one who is *inwardly* a Jew, and the real circumcision is in the heart — something not of the [law] but of the spirit. A Jew like that may not be praised by man, but he will be praised by God.

And in the Gospel of Matthew, Jesus makes a similar claim about keeping kosher, insisting once again that it is not so much the actual law the matters, but the *idea behind* the law which is truly important. In what are now famous words, the Book of Matthew (2:29) claims that Jesus said, "What goes into the mouth does not make a man unclean; it is what comes out of the mouth that makes him unclean."

Despite the Torah's clear statement that it *does* matter what we eat if we take our responsibility to holiness to heart, the early Christian tradition reads matters very differently. Thus, in the western world, in which Christianity is clearly the dominant religious tradition and culture, our conception that holiness — and chosenness — are achieved by following commandments is the perspective of only a small minority, a minority we know as the Jewish people.

At this point in our discussion, we should address one additional question: have we interpreted Paul correctly? Does this image of law reflect the way modern Christian scholars read Paul's legacy? Though we do not have the space here to dwell on this topic at length, it *is* important that we at least note that both modern Jewish *and* Christian scholars continue to read the Paulinian tradition this way. David Novak, a former faculty member at the Jewish Theological Seminary, summarizes the positions of these two religions by noting that "Christians saw [Jesus] as having fulfilled and transcended the Law . . . . Jews saw Jesus and his followers as having usurped the Law's proper power and authority . . . ."[4] Jacob Neusner, another important Jewish scholar, puts the matter in a different way:[5]

> The Christians saw Israel as a family; the Pharisees [= rabbis] saw it as a way of life. The Christians stressed their genealogy; The Pharisees their ethos and ethics. The Christian family held things in common; the holy people [= the Jews] held in common a way of life that sanctified them.

And finally, we turn to the words of Adolf von Harnack, one of the most important writers in the German Protestant Church in the late nineteenth century. Harnack wrote, "Jesus opens up to us the prospect of a union among [people], which is held together not by any legal ordinance, but by the rule of love."[6] Here, too, we see the move away from law which characterizes the works of Paul at the very beginning of Church history.

Why this Comparison Matters to Us

Before we close this chapter, it is important that we review why we decided to compare the Jewish and Christian views of commandments in the first place. What difference does it make to us as modern Jews what early Christians like Jesus and Paul apparently said?

The answer to that question lies in the fact that American society is predominantly Christian. For Israeli youth, this comparison would probably be completely irrelevant, but for those of us who live surrounded by Christian culture, the comparison *does* matter. It matters because we can now begin to understand why it sounds so strange to us to speak of observing the miẓvot as a means to holiness. Why haven't we heard that idea before? If that is such a major Jewish claim, then why does it sound so odd to us? Why does our *own* tradition seem so foreign?

The idea of expressing our unique mission through a commitment to miẓvot (both in terms of ritual *and* ethical practice) sounds so strange to us because most of the people who live in our society have been taught that one achieves holiness through *attitude*, through faith. Indeed, even many Jews now take that for granted, and fail to see how *practices* might assist us in our quest to be God's עַם סְגֻלָּה — "treasured people."

But stop, and think for a moment. If being Jewish were only about leading a moral life (not such an easy thing to do, of course) and had nothing to do with miẓvot, what would make us the unique people the Torah wants us to be? Jews and Christians both believe in God; indeed, many Jewish authorities have said that Christianity is also a monotheistic faith, worshipping but one God. Both Jews and Christians seek to live meaningful, ethical and spiritual lives, and both traditions have over the course of centuries brought to the world noble and important insights and contributions. So where do we differ?

While there are clearly many other significant differences between Judaism and Christianity, the role of law is a major one. In our society, we are often taught to see "law" and "love" as opposites; we act nobly, it is often said, either because we are "forced" to, or because we *feel* the love or commitment. "It is either one or the other," some people suggest. Often, we see on television or read of religious leaders in America who speak of the importance of love or faith, and we wonder, "where do I as a Jew fit here?" Nothing about the message seems to *contradict* Jewish tradition, but the message still *sounds* very un-Jewish. Why is that?

It is because we as Jews do not distinguish so neatly between love and law. Our tradition, beginning with some of the passages we have seen from the Torah and continuing through the rabbinic period, the liturgy and modern Jewish philosophy, has taught us that law can be the expression of love. As we saw in the *Ahavat Olam* passage, when Jews think of the mizvot, we sense God's love; when we wish to respond to that love, we do so by expressing that love through mizvot.

Isn't that often how we react with other human beings as well? [☞] Don't we usually seek to express our love for other people not only through feelings and words, but through action? And isn't it precisely that action that often helps us to realize how much other people love us? Many people can say that they love us or care for us; we usually tend to begin believing them when we see that love expressed through action, and consistent action we call commitment. Judaism claims that this interaction is true not only of human relationships, but of the relationship between people and God as well. Although most of the western world — for reasons which we now appreciate — may not work the same way, *we* understand that from the perspective of the Torah, it is our mizvot, our way of expressing concretely our love for God, that serve as our means of becoming an עַם סְגֻלָה — a people uniquely devoted to reflecting God's holiness in our world and in our society.

Questions for Discussion

1.   Do you think the effects of law are as Paul describes them? How would you feel about living in a society that did not have laws? How would you feel about a religious tradition that did not stress law?

2.   One of the facets of Conservative Judaism that differentiates it from some other movements in Judaism is its emphasis on the importance of *halakhah*, or Jewish law. Do you understand that emphasis now any differently than you did before reading this chapter? How?

3.   Think of a relationship in your life that is important to you. Would you say that that relationship is characterized by actions which are commanded? If so, what do you think would happen to that relationship if those actions were neglected? Does the analogy of such relationships to the relationship between God and the Jews make sense to you? Why?

Activities

1.   Imagine that a non-Jewish friend of yours asks you the following question: "What do Jews believe?" How would you answer? What if the friend asked you, "in what ways are Jews different from Christians?" What would you say? How would you explain the differences. What were you proud to mention? What made you uncomfortable? Do you think that such a conversations in "real life" would have been similar or very different? Why?

2.   You are a Jew living in the Galilee in the year 65 CE. A fellow Jew from your town has become part of the growing Christian community, and urges you to attend a meeting

with him. He says, "it's really a very Jewish group. We study the bible, we pray, and we want to repair the world just like the rest of the Jewish community. Come, join us!"

What will you say? Would you go? Why? How would you explain your decision to your Christian neighbors? To your Jewish neighbors?

CHAPTER FIVE:
זכור . . . אל תשכח
JEWISH TRADITION AND THE VALUE OF MEMORY

In this chapter, our second exploration of Jewish living in the context of a non-Jewish (or in North America, a Christian) world, we will focus not on the different images of law that Jews confront in their larger society, but on memory. For Jews, as for many peoples and cultures who value tradition, memory is extremely important. But as we will see, the Jewish emphasis on memory complicates our lives in a non-Jewish world for at least two reasons.

Jewish Memory in a non-Jewish World

The first reason that our emphasis on memory in a non-Jewish world is difficult is that not everyone values memory the way we do. Our North American culture often seems much more forward-oriented than it is reverent of the past. In our culture, "newer" is often seen as automatically "better." New cars, new houses, new clothes and new technology seem to interest today's modern culture. We seem much more pre-occupied with the rapid and efficient transmission of information than we are with the experience of holding in our hands a book that is several hundred years old. Many of us also like to believe that we have improved on the past, so much so that the past is either irrelevant or even dangerous. "Ancient societies' views of women," some people believe, "are so backward that we would certainly not want to emulate them." Or, perhaps, we look to generations of slavery in this country, and decide again that there is little to learn from the past.

However, Jewish tradition is a little more cynical about such advances. If the Jewish tradition could speak, it might well remind us that, while it is true that modern society has improved upon many elements of earlier societies, we have new problems. Our tradition might say that the sight of the homeless throughout our cities, the scourge of sexual harassment in the workplace and the rise of crime and drug abuse should probably give us pause as we congratulate ourselves. Furthermore, the tradition might suggest, we might well want to return to certain elements of older societies. Do we consider cities in which parents and religious organizations taught young people values too old-fashioned? Are we entirely happy with the sense that *every* dimension of our lives now seems a legitimate topic for public conversation? Are there not moments when we feel that the rapid pace of change in our society is *too* rapid, and that a return to the pace of "yesteryear" might be preferable? Jewish tradition urges us to appreciate the improvements of modernity and to seek to make even further advances; but it also reminds us that there is value in tradition for its own sake, and that if we move too quickly, we lose something even as we gain something else.

However, when we as Jews celebrate the past, study our ancestors and revere our tradition, we often find that we are somehow out of "synch" with the rest of society, and even with some of our friends, peers and neighbors.

There exists, however, a second and possibly more important reason that the Jewish emphasis on memory is difficult in a non-Jewish world. Much of what our tradition commands us to remember centers on the way we were treated by those around us; much of that memory is painful. Thus, we are caught between two difficult options. One option would be to force ourselves not to dwell on the past, and to look to the future with all its potential. The other option suggests that looking only to the future would lead us to forget our roots; too much of what we believe in, this option says, is a product of our past experiences. Painful though they may be, we need to recall them, even if doing so is disturbing and raises difficult questions for us about our non-Jewish friends and neighbors.

Which option should we select? The Torah is very explicit on the matter, and it commands us to remember and not to forget.

The Miẓvah of Zakhor

The Torah provides us with several reasons for remembering our roots, even if the memories are not always comfortable ones. One clear reason is that the Torah believes that remembering the unpleasant ways in which we were treated will make us more sensitive to those who are in now in troubling situations that *we* especially should understand. [☞] This reason is expressed perhaps most clearly in the book of Deuteronomy, or Devarim. There (in Deuteronomy 24:17-18), the Torah reminds us of this first reason for remembering:

לֹא תַטֶּה מִשְׁפַּט גֵּר יָתוֹם, וְלֹא תַחֲבֹל בֶּגֶד אַלְמָנָה. וְזָכַרְתָּ כִּי עֶבֶד הָיִיתָ בְּמִצְרַיִם וַיִּפְדְּךָ ה' אֱלֹהֶיךָ מִשָּׁם, עַל כֵּן אָנֹכִי מְצַוְּךָ לַעֲשׂוֹת אֶת הַדָּבָר הַזֶּה; "Do not undermine justice for the stranger or the orphan, and do not take a widow's garment as pawn. Rather, remember that you were a slave in the land of Egypt, and that the Lord your God rescued you from there; therefore do I command you to perform this directive." Remembering, though sometimes painful, can actually lead us to more noble action.

However, this motivation for remembering is certainly not the only reason the Torah provides us. Indeed, the most famous passage commanding us to remember, comes from the chapter following the one we quoted above and deals with the tribe of Amalek. The Torah instructs us (Deut. 25:17-19): זָכוֹר אֵת אֲשֶׁר עָשָׂה לְךָ עֲמָלֵק בַּדֶּרֶךְ בְּצֵאתְכֶם מִמִּצְרָיִם. אֲשֶׁר קָרְךָ בַּדֶּרֶךְ וַיְזַנֵּב בְּךָ כָּל הַנֶּחֱשָׁלִים אַחֲרֶיךָ וְאַתָּה עָיֵף וְיָגֵעַ . . . תִּמְחֶה אֶת זֵכֶר עֲמָלֵק מִתַּחַת הַשָּׁמָיִם, לֹא תִּשְׁכָּח; "Remember what Amalek did to you on the way as you departed Egypt. How they attacked you from the rear, [cutting down] the stragglers, when you were tired and weary. . . . [Therefore], you shall destroy the memory of Amalek from under the heaven. Do not forget." [☞]

While the Torah's command to blot out the memory of Amalek seems harsh to us, the Torah is speaking in typically ancient language, and is suggesting a simple truth: part of survival means recalling how we were once threatened. However, there is an irony here. The Torah could have simply omitted all mention of Amalek, and Amalek's memory would have been destroyed. After all, Jews are still thriving and ancient Amalek is gone! But as we'll now see, Jews have a peculiar way of destroying the memory of those who threatened us — we concentrate so hard on forgetting them that we recall them with ease!

Amalek Revisited

The story of Amalek is not over in Deuteronomy as far as Jews are concerned. Many hundreds of years after the Jews were in the desert, a descendant of the original tribe of Amalek is said to have threatened the Jews once again. This time, his name was Haman! The book of Esther claims (in Esther 3:1) that Haman was an אֲגָגִי (Agagite), and Agag was the King of the Amalekites against whom King Saul fought (I Sam. 15). Therefore, in celebrating the overthrow of Haman during our Purim festivities, our tradition claims that we are actually celebrating the destruction of Amalek, of whom the Torah had spoken centuries earlier.

But how do we "blot out" the memory of Amalek and the remembrance of Haman? We bring to services something capable of making great amounts of noise, so that each time we hear Haman's name, we can "stamp it out." However, think about what happens when we attend these services. We pay much more attention to Haman's name than anyone else's! Ironically, in making this effort to blot out Haman's memory, we spend more time looking for his name than we do thinking about the other characters of the story.

Why? Because Jews take memory seriously. Even though we understand the threat that Amalek or Haman may have been to us, and even though we respond by promising to "blot out" their memories, we actually focus on them consistently. Beneath the surface of our bravado and our promises to extinguish their memories, we know we cannot afford to do that. To forget those events of our past would be to forget our origins. And we hope that recalling those roots will not only cause us to live more ethical and caring lives, it will also lead us to a commitment to protect ourselves and future generations of Jews.

Amalek of the Twentieth Century?

We see that phenomenon at work in yet another context as well. Many of us probably have grandparents, parents or teachers who, when they utter Hitler's name, follow the name with the Hebrew phrase יִמַּח שְׁמוֹ, or "may his memory be destroyed." Again, we have to wonder if what we say is what we really want! Do we really want Hitler's name obliterated? If we do, why do we insist on teaching our students and our children about the tragedy of the Sho'ah? We cannot have it both ways. Either we will blot out the memory by forgetting the entire episode, or we must remember the tragedy, and in so doing, keep the memory of those who have attacked us alive.

Before we move on, a brief word on the terminology of Sho'ah is in order. Throughout this discussion, and in discussions which will follow, this Sourcebook consciously avoids the use of the term "Holocaust." Holocaust is an English word which means "burnt offering" or "sacrifice to God." The Jews of Europe in the 1930's and 1940's were not sacrificed — they were murdered. There is a tremendous difference; this Sourcebook uses the word Sho'ah in order to take that difference seriously. That, too, is part of the responsibility of remembering.

But let's return to the central discussion of this chapter. Our tradition does not want us to have it both ways, and it does not believe that we have a real choice. Ultimately, if we are to be faithful to our roots and to our unique role in the world, Jewish tradition says, we *remember* where we have come from. We must recall our slavery at the Passover seder, so much so that the Haggadah says that בְּכָל דּוֹר וָדוֹר חַיָּב אָדָם לִרְאוֹת אֶת עַצְמוֹ כְּאִלּוּ הוּא יָצָא מִמִּצְרָיִם — "in each and every generation, a person is obligated to see himself (or herself) as if he (or she) personally came out of Egypt." We must also recall the martyrdom of our rabbis as we recite אֵלֶּה אֶזְכְּרָה (*Eileh Ezkerah*, or "the Martyrology") on Yom Kippur afternoon, the narrowly avoided tragedy of the Jews in Shushan on Purim, and the destruction that was tragically *not* averted in Germany and the rest of Europe both on Yom Ha-Sho'ah (Sho'ah Memorial Day) and throughout our schooling. It is not that we yearn to dwell on the unfortunate tragedies of our past; it is simply that we recognize that too much of who we are is related to those experiences. If we forget them, we lose part of ourselves. If we ignore them, we risk allowing them to repeat. If we overlook them, we fail the mizvah of Zakhor.

But this sort of remembering is not easy. It is painful for us, and it can offend those who live around us. "Why can't you just move on," our non-Jewish friends will often say; and it *can* be uncomfortable to live primarily among non-Jewish people and insist on recalling all these events. How do *you* feel when you meet someone from Germany who you realize must have been alive in the 1940's, or whose parents must have lived then? Many of us feel very uncomfortable. We would like to see this person as any other human being, and yet we find ourselves unable to do so. The Torah, in the passages we cited above, suggests that this discomfort is probably healthy. But that does not make it easy. It only reminds us of our unique place in this world, and of the challenges and responsibilities that being Jewish carries with it.

Questions for Discussion

1. Is the miẓvah of zakhor still applicable today? How should we react to threats of anti-semitism today? How should we react when others are threatened by prejudice? Is it even *possible* to live in the North America today if we insist on remembering? What about Germany or Spain?

2. Are there modern "Amalekites" today? Do you believe that there are people whose evil we must promise never to forget? How would you treat those people? How should we perform the miẓvah of זָכוֹר (*zakhor*) today?

3. Most of us have parents and grandparents who were alive during the years of the Sho'ah, in the 1930's and 1940's. Often, their views of Germany in particular and the non-Jewish world in general have been profoundly impacted by their experiences and their memory. Do you believe that your parents or grandparents fulfill the miẓvah of *zakhor* differently than you do? Are you comfortable with their way of thinking about the non-Jewish world? Why? Why not?

4. Are there issues — either specifically Jewish or not — which you think we need to remember more than we do? Can you think of ways in which the Jewish tradition could *help* you accomplish that remembering?

5. Do you think that Jews encourage anti-semitism by focusing too often on the past? Why? Why not? What, if anything, do you think we should change?

Activities

You might put the command of remembering "on trial." Appoint a "prosecutor" to argue that remembering is no longer necessary, and indeed, is guilty of causing a variety of negative impacts on those who remember "too much." A defense will also be necessary, to argue that remembering is crucial. Jurors will have to weigh the arguments made by each side. Does remembering actually make us more sensitive to the difficult situations of others today, or does it just make us bitter? Are there *certain things* we are better off not remembering? How will the jury vote?

Notes and Comments

CHAPTER SIX
אור לגוים
"A LIGHT UNTO THE NATIONS"

In the previous chapter, we discussed the importance that our tradition places upon memory. We saw that from a Jewish perspective, memory is important even when it is painful. Memory, we suggested in that discussion, is part of what it takes to survive. A people needs to be realistic about its past if it is to successfully guide its future. We have an obligation in Jewish *law* to recall Amalek and all that they did to our ancestors. Such memory may sometimes seem discouraging, but it is necessary nonetheless.

Yet our discussion also pointed to an additional function of memory. We saw that the commandment of *zakhor* is designed not to make us bitter about life or the world in which we live, but to enable us to become more sensitive to life and to our world. If we can recall the depth of our own feelings at being mistreated or forgotten, we may well be able to react more effectively to assist other people in the world who also need protection. That is why our memory of the Jewish people's slavery in Egypt is so important. [☞] The verse we cited in the last chapter bears repeating here. The Torah reminds us that our own experience *must* impact the types of living experiences we create for other people. As we saw, the Torah admonishes us: לֹא תַטֶּה מִשְׁפַּט גֵּר יָתוֹם, וְלֹא תַחֲבֹל בֶּגֶד אַלְמָנָה. וְזָכַרְתָּ כִּי עֶבֶד הָיִיתָ בְּמִצְרַיִם וַיִּפְדְּךָ ה' אֱלֹהֶיךָ מִשָּׁם, עַל כֵּן אָנֹכִי מְצַוְּךָ לַעֲשׂוֹת אֶת הַדָּבָר הַזֶּה; "Do not undermine justice for the stranger or the orphan, and do not take a widow's garment as pawn. Rather, remember that you were a slave in the land of Egypt, and that the Lord your God rescued you from there; therefore do I command you to perform this directive." Remembering well should lead to living well. As we will now see, this instance of reminding us of the importance of our history in Egypt is not unique in the Torah. In fact, the Torah reminds us often of our years in Egypt, so that we become healers, and not new Pharaohs.

For You Were Slaves in the Land of Egypt

It is not enough, the Torah suggests, for our experience of slavery to impact on how we treat free people like widows and strangers. Important as *that* miẓvah may be, Jews are assigned an even more ambitious goal — we are commanded to change the very nature of slavery itself. That change began with our treatment of Jews who had to sell themselves into slavery in order to pay back debts. In Devarim (Deut. 15:12-15), the Torah commands us: כִּי יִמָּכֵר לְךָ אָחִיךָ הָעִבְרִי אוֹ הָעִבְרִיָּה וַעֲבָדְךָ שֵׁשׁ שָׁנִים, וּבַשָּׁנָה הַשְּׁבִיעִת תְּשַׁלְּחֶנּוּ חָפְשִׁי מֵעִמָּךְ. וְכִי תְשַׁלְּחֶנּוּ חָפְשִׁי מֵעִמָּךְ, לֹא תְשַׁלְּחֶנּוּ רֵיקָם. הַעֲנֵיק תַּעֲנִיק לוֹ מִצֹּאנְךָ וּמִגָּרְנְךָ וּמִיִּקְבֶךָ, אֲשֶׁר בֵּרַכְךָ ה' אֱלֹקֶיךָ תִּתֶּן לוֹ. וְזָכַרְתָּ כִּי עֶבֶד הָיִיתָ בְּאֶרֶץ מִצְרַיִם; "If a fellow Hebrew, man or woman, is sold to you, he shall serve you six years, and in the seventh year you shall set him free. When you set him free, do not let him go empty-handed. Provide him from the flock, threshing floor and vat, with which the Lord your God has blessed you. Bear in mind that you were slaves in the land of Egypt."

Of course, the Torah knows of two sorts of slaves — Jewish slaves and non-Jewish slaves. And although the laws in this section apply only to Jewish slaves, and even these laws do not do away with slavery completely (though the rabbis later did take steps to render the Jewish practice of slavery effectively impossible), we must not lose sight of what a tremendous advance these *halakhot* (Jewish laws) represented in the ancient world. The very idea that if one had the luxury of the services of another human, one had to remember that the laborer was *human*, that you could not *own* laborers (and therefore had to free them on the seventh year) and that even when you freed them, your responsibilities for them were not completed. Jews were required to liberate these people with some possessions, so that they would not begin life in abject poverty all over again, and so that they could hopefully avoid becoming slaves again. Why did Jews have to go so far for these "slaves?" Because, the Torah reminds us, we were slaves in Egypt, and we, better than anyone else, should know how destructive slavery is of human dignity. We, therefore, must be the first to begin to alter the very way that slavery is practiced.

Yet this attitude is not limited to slaves alone. Even people who are free, but who are strangers in our society (and are therefore likely to be taken advantage of) are our responsibility. In the book of Va-Yikra (Leviticus) the Torah expands the list of those whom we must be careful not to exploit. There, we read: וְכִי יָגוּר אִתְּךָ גֵר בְּאַרְצְכֶם, לֹא תוֹנוּ אֹתוֹ. כְּאֶזְרָח מִכֶּם יִהְיֶה לָכֶם הַגֵּר הַגָּר אִתְּכֶם וְאָהַבְתָּ לוֹ כָּמוֹךָ כִּי גֵרִים הֱיִיתֶם בְּאֶרֶץ מִצְרָיִם, אֲנִי ה' אֱלֹקֵיכֶם;

"³³When a stranger resides with you in your land, you shall not wrong him. ³⁴The stranger who resides with you shall be to you as one of your citizens; you shall love him as yourself, for you were strangers in the land of Egypt: I the Lord am your God."

And that is not enough! The Torah goes even further. Our tradition claims that our past as slaves should impact not only our treatment of the downtrodden such as widows, strangers and slaves, but the way we do business on a day to day basis as well. Our everyday sense of right and wrong must also be informed by the lessons we learned from being slaves. The previous passage about the treatment of strangers continues with verse 35 and reads: לֹא תַעֲשׂוּ עָוֶל בַּמִּשְׁפָּט, בַּמִּדָּה בַּמִּשְׁקָל וּבַמְּשׂוּרָה. מֹאזְנֵי צֶדֶק אַבְנֵי צֶדֶק אֵיפַת צֶדֶק וְהִין צֶדֶק יִהְיֶה לָכֶם, אֲנִי ה' אֱלֹקֵיכֶם אֲשֶׁר הוֹצֵאתִי אֶתְכֶם מֵאֶרֶץ מִצְרָיִם; "³⁵You shall not falsify measures of length, weight, or capacity. ³⁶You shall have an honest balance, honest weights, an honest *ephah*-measure, and an honest *hin*-measure. I the Lord am your God who freed you from the land of Egypt." To have been redeemed from Egypt, our tradition says, is to recognize that God's ultimate vision for our world is one in which all human interactions are characterized by justice and fairness. Recognizing that God has redeemed us from Egypt must even lead to conclusions about the way we conduct our financial affairs, and indeed, all our interpersonal relations. Another section of the Torah (Deuteronomy 24) even goes so far as to suggest that our farming techniques should be influenced by our past as slaves. There, the Torah commands: כִּי תִבְצֹר כַּרְמְךָ לֹא תְעוֹלֵל אַחֲרֶיךָ, לַגֵּר לַיָּתוֹם וְלָאַלְמָנָה יִהְיֶה. וְזָכַרְתָּ כִּי עֶבֶד הָיִיתָ בְּאֶרֶץ מִצְרָיִם; "²¹When you gather the grapes of your vineyard, do not pick it over again; that shall go to the stranger, the fatherless, and the widow. ²²Always remember that you were a slave in the land of Egypt . . . ."

What do all these verses that we have cited have in common? They link the command that we behave in a certain way due to our past experience of national suffering. We should know, our tradition insists, how painful it feels to be the victim of injustice. We, therefore, must avoid *causing* injustice at all costs. We have seen, the Torah suggests, the power of God's redemption in history; therefore, we must become the agents of continuing that redemption, and must serve as a means for bringing about the betterment of the world in which we live. [☞]

From National Redemption to Or La-Goyim

But as we have mentioned throughout the discussions in previous chapters, Jews are a very small minority of the world's population. How, then, can our own actions actually make a difference in the broader world picture? What effect will *our* actions actually have?

This important question is not at all a new one. For quite some time, our tradition has spoken not only of the Jew's responsibility to act decently, but of a second responsibility, to serve as a model for *other people's* actions. This responsibility appears in our tradition as far back as our prophets, more than twenty-five hundred years ago. In a world very different from our own, Isaiah already tells the Jewish people that God has an important message for them on this subject. God says (Is. 42:6): אֲנִי ה' קְרָאתִיךָ בְצֶדֶק וְאַחְזֵק בְּיָדֶךָ, וְאֶצָּרְךָ וְאֶתֶּנְךָ לִבְרִית עָם לְאוֹר גּוֹיִם; "I, God, have called you to serve the cause of justice; I have held you by the hand and created you, and I have made you as a covenant of the people and a light [to the] nations."

Notice what God says in this passage. The verse seems to imply that the very reason for which we were created was to serve the cause of justice, or to be a model to the other nations of the world in repairing the world. This "call to arms" has been a powerful rallying cry throughout Jewish history. For hundreds of years, many Jews have heeded this call and the call of our other prophets to be representatives of the cause of justice in society. In North America and in Israel, in political and cultural contexts, Isaiah's call seems to have been heeded by Jews of all different walks of life.

Many of us may have been told by our grandparents of their involvement with political groups that sought to help the "underdogs" in our society. In the United States, the association of the Jewish vote with the Democratic party was for many years beyond question. The Democratic Party, which early in this century carved out for itself the role of protecting the weak in society, attracted many Jews who heard echoes of the prophets in that party's agenda. Statistically, it is also very likely that many of our grandparents were either involved with or sympathetic to socialist enterprises. Jews in North America were often sympathetic to a socialist vision of the world, for socialists argued that radical changes in the way society distributed goods and economic power were necessary. Where would Jews get such an idea? In some respects, some of the very core ideas of socialism seem to be reflected in the Torah itself.

In the book of Deuteronomy, the Torah reviews the concept of the sabbatical year, and tells us that every seven years, a major adjustment of economic power had to occur. The Torah commands (Deut. 15:1-2): מִקֵּץ שֶׁבַע שָׁנִים תַּעֲשֶׂה שְׁמִטָּה. וְזֶה דְּבַר הַשְּׁמִטָּה שָׁמוֹט כָּל בַּעַל מַשֵּׁה יָדוֹ אֲשֶׁר יַשֶּׁה בְּרֵעֵהוּ, לֹא יִגֹּשׂ אֶת רֵעֵהוּ וְאֶת אָחִיו כִּי קָרָא שְׁמִטָּה לַה׳; "¹Every seventh year you must cancel debts. This is how *shemittah* must work: every person who is owed money must give up his claim against his neighbor. ²He must not require payment [of the debt] from his neighbor and his brother, for God has commanded the *shemittah* year." According to the Torah, then, if people owed money, their debt was cancelled when the *shemittah* year arrived. The Torah, it seems, sought to break the cycle of poverty in which those who borrowed money often found themselves trapped. Socialist leaders, of course, did not quote the Torah in their writings; but does it not appear that many Jews who learned of the agenda of socialism found it appealing precisely because it seemed to reflect the ideals and commitments of their most sacred writings.

Although many elements of our society have changed, many Jews in the United States have since given their allegiance to other political parties and socialism has begun to fade as a result of the cruel and oppressive communist regimes in Europe, it is important that we recall that the Jewish people is still responsible for one of the boldest socialist experiments in the world today — the kibbutz movement. The kibbutz movement began as an attempt to create an entirely new form of society. The founders of Israel's earliest *kibbutzim* hoped to create a society in which the distinction between rich and poor did not exist and where people lived with the daily sense of responsibility for all members of their community. [☞] The kibbutz movement has also changed since Israel's early years, but at its core, much of its mission remains the same. It is one of the modern-day Jewish responses to the calls of Leviticus, Deuteronomy and Isaiah to make the act of Jewish living a process of healing our world and of encouraging others to do the same.

Jews have heeded those call in a variety of fashions. Many of us have seen the famous photographs of Rabbi Abraham Joshua Heschel (whose writings we quoted in Chapter One) marching with Dr. Martin Luther King, Jr., on behalf of African-American rights. Dr. Heschel, of course, was a profoundly knowledgeable and committed Jew. But many observers have also pointed out that some Jews participate in the process of repairing the world — which we call תִּיקוּן עוֹלָם, or *tikkun olam* — even if they are not outwardly observant or Jewishly involved. This was true of many of the leaders of the socialist movement, the movements in North American and Israel to improve the treatment of women in society and in other important causes as well. Professor Yosef Hayim Yerushalmi, of Columbia University, refers to this sort of Jew as a "psychological Jew," and says that psychological Jews are:[7]

> those . . . [who show] no special need to define themselves as Jews or to embrace any particular form of Jewish commitment, but who have felt themselves to be somehow irreducibly Jewish nonetheless. . . . Alienated from classic Jewish texts, Psychological Jews tend to insist on inalienable Jewish traits. Intellectuality and independence of mind, the highest of ethical and moral standards, concern for social justice . . . — these are among the qualities they will claim, if called upon, as quintessentially Jewish.

It would not be fair, of course, to suggest that socialism, feminism or other similar political movements are *Jewish* movements. Many crucial contributions to these movements have been made by non-Jewish men and women. But at the forefront of each of these movements were Jews, who whatever their level of commitment to Jewish life and community, seem to have been profoundly influenced by their Jewish roots. Could this be the fulfillment of Isaiah's dream that Jews would serve as בְּרִית עָם לְאוֹר גּוֹיִם, a convenantal community which acts as a model for the other nations? And let's not let our discussion of Jews as models for the remainder of the world end here. Many North American Jews believe that one of Israel's crucial roles as a state is to show the rest of the world how a government and military can act morally, with devotion to citizens of all colors and creeds, both within and sometimes outside of its borders. Some of us believe that Israel *should* act this way, while others believe that Israel *does* act this way. But regardless of which group we feel a part, most of us know what it is like to feel tremendous pride when Israel sets an example of courage, tolerance or openness. We ourselves are proud when non-Jews point to Israel as a model of development, modernity or some other quality which merits wide-spread respect. We find ourselves resonating to the words of Justice Louis D. Brandeis, a Jewish member of the United States Supreme Court, who wrote:[8]

I find Jews possessed of those very qualities which we of the twentieth century seek to develop in our struggle for justice and democracy: a deep moral feeling which makes them capable of noble acts; a deep sense of the brotherhood of [humankind]; . . . These experiences have made me feel that the Jewish people have something which should be saved for the world . . .

What, exactly, is that "something" that the Jews have which should be saved for the world?

What are the causes that the Jewish tradition would have us take upon ourselves at the start of the twenty-first century that will show us as model, that will make us an אוֹר גּוֹיִם? Are we comfortable with the idea of playing that role? Where do we start?

Questions for Discussion

1. When Jews pray in the morning, they recite the following blessing before the *amidah*, at the most crucial part of the service: בָּרוּךְ אַתָּה ה' גָּאַל יִשְׂרָאֵל, "Praised are You, Lord, Redeemer of Israel." Now that you have studied this chapter, which "redemption" to you think the blessing is referring to? Why do you think the creators of our liturgy felt that redemption was so important that they placed this blessing immediately before the most important part of the service?

2. Is Israel a *unique* country with a "higher" commitment to acting morally? Is such a belief amongst non-Jews the reason that Israel is always in the news in North America, even in communities with few Jews? Is holding Israel to such a high standard healthy for the Jewish people?

3. This chapter has made much of our responsibility to learn from our past, and to make sure that we help protect others who might fall into similar situations. Who are the "slaves" of today? How could you help them?

4. Do you feel that Jews and African-Americans still share a partnership because of our shared experiences of slavery, or do you think that the alliance symbolized by Dr. Heschel's marching with Dr. King has ended? How do you explain whatever changes you believe have taken place? Should we simply accept those changes, or is there something we can/should do to alter the situation?

5. What is the most serious problem facing our community today? How can you get involved to help solve it?

Activities

1. You are a major leader in your Jewish community, and a well respected member of the community at large. A long-time supporter of Israel, you are proud that the Jewish state has always tried to live up to what you believe is a higher standard of action than many other countries. But now, the news is filled with details of a series of incidents in which Israeli authorities have behaved in ways which you think do not live up to the responsibility of being an אוֹר לַגּוֹיִם (*or la-goyim*, a "light unto the nations"). You decide to convene a meeting of the heads of the major Jewish organizations in your community. What course of action do you recommend? [Appoint several other committee members, and see where the conversation heads ...]

Notes and Comments

CHAPTER SEVEN:
אם אין אני לי מי לי
OUR OBLIGATION TO SAFEGUARD JEWISH INTERESTS

In the previous chapter, we discovered that, although our tradition encourages us to maintain a noticeable difference between ourselves and our neighbors, it also urges us to be part of the larger society in which we live, work, learn and socialize. Thus, although the first chapters of this Sourcebook pointed to the importance of our creating a distinction between ourselves and other communities by observing different religious practices and keeping a sense of our unique purpose as Jews, the principle of אוֹר לַגּוֹיִם (*or la-goyim*, "a light unto the nations) insists that we, as Jews, have something valuable to share with those around us.

However, we need to note something about this concept of אוֹר לַגּוֹיִם. Nothing about this part of our tradition acknowledges that our interests and those of our non-Jewish neighbors may well be at odds with each other. Nothing about the concept of אוֹר לַגּוֹיִם implies that the nations of the world are in any way deprived because we play this role; indeed, precisely the opposite is the case! Our tradition claims that our role as a "light unto the nations" actually benefits those around us. This is true of all the principles at which we've looked thus far; none of them seem to recognize the fact that there might arise conflict between our needs and the interests of those around us.

Yet all of us who live in societies that are largely not Jewish know very well that life is not always that simple. Many of us have had the uncomfortable feeling that life can sometimes be more complicated than simply insisting upon our own uniqueness and at the same time contributing to the world around us. Often, we sense that these two ideals are in conflict; that realization can make us extraordinarily uncomfortable. [☞]

The conflict between creating a unique role for ourselves and serving as a leader in the world emerges in a variety of ways. Sometimes, as we will see particularly in the next chapter, we are concerned about the appearance of what is commonly called "dual loyalty," or our commitment to both our own government and the State of Israel, or the citizens of our own country and Jews throughout the world. For many Jews, events of the Persian Gulf War in 1991 brought this issue to the fore. Imagine the following only slightly hypothetical scenario: how should we react if during a war in which the United States is involved, the interests of the United States and those of Israel do not mesh? Should Jews urge a "diversion" of U.S. warplanes to hunt for Iraqi scud missiles aimed at Israel, even if the United States State Department or Pentagon claims that those planes are desperately needed for other purposes and that scud missiles are too inexact to cause a serious threat to Israel?

At other times, our concern arises not from the issue of "dual loyalties," but from confusion about how to divide up our resources: in a world in which there are more legitimate needs for our tzedakah than we could possibly satisfy, whom do we serve first? Should all our money go to Jewish causes (because we believe that no one else will support the Jewish causes) or should our money be divided? Should, perhaps, *all* our money be given to the cause of the most needy, even if that means that *none* of it goes to Jewish groups? What does our tradition say about *these* types of situations? How are we to respond? Does being an אוֹר לַגּוֹיִם mandate a particular answer to this question? Can being so concerned with serving as an אוֹר לַגּוֹיִם sometimes undermine our commitment to *Jewish* needs?

We will divide our discussion of these concerns into two sections. In this chapter, we will introduce three sources about this issue and begin to ponder their possible application to a variety of dilemmas that we might feel. In Chapter Eight, we will look more closely at some actual instances to see how different Jews balanced the tension between caring about uniquely Jewish concerns and living as part of a larger social or national group. Thus, we begin in this chapter with the theoretical approaches to the issue, and in the next chapter will look at some concrete examples. Let's begin now with the theory.

Two Rabbinic Sources on the Limits of Self-Interest

The first source we'll examine is perhaps the most well known. It is also instructive because it implicitly suggests that there are no easy guidelines for how to make decisions in cases such as these. The tradition quotes this passage (Pirkei Avot 1:14) in the name of Hillel:

הוּא הָיָה אוֹמֵר: אִם אֵין אֲנִי לִי, מִי לִי? וּכְשֶׁאֲנִי לְעַצְמִי, מָה אֲנִי? וְאִם לֹא עַכְשָׁו אֵמָתָי?;

"[Hillel] used to say: If I am not [careful in looking out] for myself, who [will be so careful to watch out] for me? If I am [only] for myself, what [kind of person] am I? And if not now, when?"

What did Hillel have in mind when he uttered these words? Certain commentators believe that Hillel was addressing primarily the issue of personal improvement and spiritual growth. While that is possible, Jews have cited this passage in numerous contexts since Hillel uttered it almost two thousand years ago. Regardless of what Hillel originally meant, the phrase has become a virtual maxim for Jews everywhere; but for a maxim, it is not especially helpful! It is not as helpful as we might have hoped it would be because it reminds us that ideal action on our part can be neither completely selfish, nor wholly unselfish. How do we ultimately create a balance? Perhaps we can derive some additional benefit from another source.

The Babylonian Talmud (Bava Meẓia 71a), recognizes that we will never have enough resources to assist all those in need, and it offers the following "formula" for creating priorities: תָּנֵי רַב יוֹסֵף: "אִם כֶּסֶף תַּלְוֶה אֶת עַמִּי אֶת הֶעָנִי עִמָּךְ (שְׁמוֹת כב:כד)" — עַמִּי וְנָכְרִי עַמִּי קוֹדֵם. עָנִי וְעָשִׁיר, עָנִי קוֹדֵם. עֲנִייָּךְ וַעֲנִיֵּי עִירְךָ, עֲנִייָּךְ קוֹדְמִין. עֲנִיֵּי עִירְךָ וַעֲנִיֵּי עִיר אַחֶרֶת, עֲנִיֵּי עִירְךָ קוֹדְמִין; Rav Yosef taught: [The Torah teaches, in Exodus 22:24)], "If you lend money to My people, to the poor among you . . . ."[9] [From this we learn that if your decision is whether to give to] My people or a non-Jewish person, My people comes first. [Between] a poor person and a wealthy person, the poor person comes first. Your [own] poor [i.e., the poor of your family] and the poor of your city, your [own] poor come first. [Between] the poor of your city and the poor of another city, the poor of your city come first."

Rav Yosef bases his midrash, or the conclusion he derives from this verse, upon the style of the Torah's language here. He understands that the Torah could have said simply, "If you lend money to people, do not act toward them as a creditor: exact no interest from them." However, the Torah says more than that, and adds the phrase אֶת עַמִּי, אֶת הֶעָנִי עִמָּךְ. The entire verse now reads: "If you lend money to *My people, to the poor among you*, do not act toward them as a creditor: exact no interest from them." Why, Rav Yosef seems to ask, are these words part of the verse? They must be there to teach us something in addition to the prohibition on taking interest. Their role must be to instruct us about the priorities for lending this money.

The Sifrei, a rabbinic commentary on the book of Devarim (Deuteronomy) continues this line of reasoning even further, and adds: יוֹשְׁבֵי הָאָרֶץ קוֹדְמִין לְיוֹשְׁבֵי חוּ"ל, "inhabitants of the land of Israel take precedence over inhabitants of other lands."[10] Finally, there are views that יוֹשְׁבֵי יְרוּשָׁלַיִם קוֹדְמִין לְיוֹשְׁבֵי עָרִים אֲחֵרוֹת שֶׁבְּאֶרֶץ יִשְׂרָאֵל, or "the inhabitants of Jerusalem take precedence over the inhabitants of other cities in the land of Israel."[11]

Before moving on to a third perspective on אִם אֵין אֲנִי לִי מִי לִי, we need to ask ourselves a few questions about these passages. How comfortable are we with this perspective? Are we as convinced as the Sifrei seems to be that these kinds of questions can be reduced to neat formulae? Do we agree that all our charitable funds should be given to Jews if we do not have enough for everyone? Do we agree that causes in Israel should be supported first, even if that might mean that other Jewish communities would not receive funding? And what counts as "our city" today? Television and modern communications have had a profound impact on what seems "local" to us; we are often much more aware of suffering in other countries throughout the world than we are of the hungry and homeless in our local area. Should this impact our decisions?

Furthermore, we need to ask about the apparent contradiction between Hillel's position and Rav Yosef's position. The second part of Hillel's phrase, which we will examine again in the next chapter, asks וּכְשֶׁאֲנִי לְעַצְמִי, מָה אֲנִי?, or "when I am only for myself, what am I?" Rav Yosef's position does not seem terribly concerned with that issue. How do we explain that? On the surface, we might argue (correctly) that Rav Yosef is speaking specifically of tzedakah, or charity, while Hillel may have something much less tangible in mind. But let's ignore that distinction temporarily. Which perspective seems more moral? Which seems more realistic? Which makes you more (or less) nervous or uncomfortable?

When you come across a position like Rav Yosef's, do you feel uncomfortable? Would you be willing to teach a public lesson in your High School based on Rav Yosef's position? Many of us would find ourselves extremely ill at ease in such a setting. Why? Interestingly, the last source which we'll examine in this chapter suggests that it is time for North American Jews to somehow move beyond these feelings of discomfort.

A More Contemporary Position

Alan Dershowitz, a well known civil libertarian and law professor at Harvard University, and the author of a book entitled *Chutzpah*, believes passionately that Jews are much too nervous about asserting and protecting our own interests in North America. We will examine material from his book in future chapters, but for the present, let's look at the book's opening and closing comments. Dershowitz begins his volume with the following very clear statement:[12]

> American Jews need more chutzpah. Notwithstanding the stereotype, we are not pushy or assertive enough for our own good and for the good of our more vulnerable brothers and sisters in other parts of the world. Despite our apparent success, deep down we see ourselves as second-class citizens — as guests in another people's land. We worry about charges of dual loyalty, of being too rich, too smart, and too powerful. Our cautious leaders obsess about what the "real" Americans will think of us. We don't appreciate how much we have contributed to the greatness of this country and don't accept that we are entitled to first-class status in this diverse and heterogeneous democracy.

The majority of Dershowitz' book is a description of major events, most of them relatively recent, in which Jews have failed to assert themselves sufficiently (at least in Dershowitz' opinion). But at the conclusion of the his book, he leaves us with a profound challenge:

> Pogo once said: "We have seen the enemy and he is *us*!" As Jews, we have not yet been given the luxury of seeing ourselves as the enemy. There are still too many external enemies who challenge the very physical survival of the Jewish people in Israel and through the world. But as we become stronger in the face of our external enemies, we must prepare to confront ourselves. As *Jewish* Americans, are we prepared to demand the first-class status we have earned in America that we have helped others to move toward? As *American* Jews, are we prepared to insist on being treated as first-class Jews, rather than as exiles from our only true and normal home, Israel? The answer to these questions in largely, if not entirely, in our own hands. One conclusion is certain: unless we regard ourselves as first-class Americans and as first-class Jews, no one else will so regard us. [☞]

Those are extremely powerful words, and as his book makes clear, Dershowitz is a passionate believer in that position. But what about אוֹר לַגּוֹיִם? Will that fit with Dershowitz' position? Which is more important? Need they be in conflict? And how will we balance the conflict? The truth is, perhaps the most important thing for us to realize about this conflict is that it exists, and that it defies easy resolution. More important than figuring out a neat solution to this challenge is our realization as Jews that we will confront this dilemma, and that part of being a thoughtful and committed Jew in a largely non-Jewish society is having had some experience in thinking the issue through in a sophisticated and open-minded way. That may not actually "solve" the dilemma, but it may well do more than neat solutions would to prepare us to live meaningfully as Jews and responsibly as citizens of a larger world.

Questions for Discussion

1. Have there been times when you felt that you did not stand up strongly enough for a Jewish cause? What was the situation? Why, in retrospect, do you think you responded the way you did? Do you think you would respond differently in the future? What has changed in you?

2. How comfortable do you think you would be arguing for the case made by Professor Dershowitz in front of a group of students at your High School? What would you be feeling as you made that case? How do you think they would respond? How does *that* make you feel?

Activities

1. Chapter Six of this Sourcebook addressed the importance of serving as an אוֹר לַגּוֹיִם (*or la-goyim*, a "light unto the nations"). This chapter has dwelled on our obligation to protect Jewish interests. Can you think of instances in which those two ideals might be in conflict with each other? Make a list of those instances . . . . What do they have in common? How would you react in each of those cases? Would your reactions in each case be the same? Why?

2. A candidate in your community running for national office has an excellent record on domestic issues. You genuinely believe that this candidate is by far the best choice to address some of the serious social problems that your community faces. But this candidate has a record of not being nearly as supportive of Israel as you think should have been the case. The opponent, a person you believe is much less talented and is less qualified for the position, has a strong record in support of Israel. Now, the local newspaper in your city contacts you. The editor explains that the paper would like a

letter written by a leading member of the Jewish community (you, of course!) sharing a viewpoint on how Jews should react.

Do you agree to write the letter? If you do, what do you say? What will happen if you don't write the letter? What are you concerned might occur if you *do* write the letter? Try writing such a letter. . . .

CHAPTER EIGHT
כשאני לעצמי מה אני
THREE JEWS WHO FACED HILLEL'S DILEMMA

When it comes to balancing our own self-interest with our commitment to larger causes, it seems that Hillel and the Sifrei on Deuteronomy disagree. Alan Dershowitz, as we saw at the end of the previous chapter, adds yet another dimension to the conversation. In this chapter, we will explore this issue further by looking at three actual examples of what Jews did or did not do around the time of the second World War. Two of the examples deal with how the United States might have assisted Jews during the Sho'ah, while the third deals with President Truman's decision to recognize the State of Israel. In two of the cases, we know exactly what the Jews in question said and did not say, while in the third, we can only guess. Throughout, we can see not only the three Jewish figures involved, but ourselves and our own confusion as to how we would act in these sorts of cases. The point of this chapter is not to condemn those who came before us for their possible errors or shortcomings, or even to applaud those who took courageous stands, though they certainly deserve praise. Rather, the purpose is to ask ourselves how their experiences might inform our own choices should we ever have to make them.

Cordell Hull and Nahum Goldmann

The first of our cases involves the United States Secretary of State during World War II, a man named Cordell Hull. Hull, a long-time Democrat from Tennessee, was himself not Jewish, though he was married to a Jewish woman. In 1940, after a boat carrying Jewish refugees who had escaped from France was turned away from Mexico and ordered to return to Europe where the Jews were certain to die, the boat stopped for fuel in Norfolk, Virginia. Dr. Nahum Goldmann, a North American Zionist of great importance, went to see Secretary of State Hull to ask that the Jewish refugees be allowed to stay in the United States. Secretary Hull, married to a Jewish woman, pointed to an American flag in his office and told Goldmann, "I took an oath to protect that flag and obey the laws of my country and you are asking me to break those laws." [☞]

However, Dr. Goldmann was not easily silenced. He understood that, if the Jewish refugees were not allowed entry into the United States, they would certainly die. He reminded Hull that, a few weeks earlier, some German sailors who were opposed to Hitler had jumped overboard as their ship left New York, and since the United States was not yet officially at war with Germany, the Coast Guard had given those soldiers sanctuary at Ellis Island. Goldmann sarcastically requested that Hull send the Jewish refugees a telegram suggesting that they jump overboard, so that they would be treated no worse than the German soldiers who were given protection. Hull became infuriated by Goldmann's sarcasm, and responded, "Dr. Goldmann, you are the most cynical man I have ever met." When Goldmann retorted, "I ask you, Mr. Secretary, who is the cynical one — I who wish to save these innocent people or you who are prepared to send them back to their death," Hull dismissed Goldmann from his office and refused to even shake his hand.[13]

In the end, Eleanor Roosevelt interceded on behalf of the refugees, and they were allowed entry into the United States. But had it not been for her, Secretary Hull would have had them sent back to Europe! It is disturbing enough for those of us who are citizens of the United States that this was the policy of our government during such an important period for our people. To make matters worse, we are forced to ask a different question. Where was Mrs. Hull during these months? What did this Jewish woman, who was certainly in a position to influence at least the Secretary of State, do on behalf of her people? Did she insist that her husband change his mind and allow the Jews to enter her country, or did she simply hope that the matter would not become more embarrassing, and that the presence of these refugees would not make her situation even less comfortable with time? Were her fellow-Jews simply a "problem" that she hoped would go away?

Mrs. Hull, as our tradition makes clear, was not the first Jewish woman married to a non-Jewish man who had this opportunity to help her people. The book of Esther, which we read each Purim and which we'll discuss again in our next chapter, tells us that when Haman threatened the lives of the Jews of Shushan, Mordecai urged her to intercede on their behalf with the King Ahasuerus. But Esther refused, claiming that if she approached the king without being invited, she might be killed. Mordecai, like Dr. Goldmann, had a response; in his case, it was a response that has become a classic. As many of us are aware from our reading of this story on Purim, Mordechai said to Esther (Esth. 4:14): וּמִי יוֹדֵעַ אִם לְעֵת כָּזֹאת הִגַּעַתְּ לַמַּלְכוּת, "[For if you are silent now, help and deliverance will come to the Jews from another place, but you and your father's house will be destroyed.] And who knows if it is for this kind of moment that you have come to [your position] in the kingdom?"

Mordecai's question is as appropriate for us as it was for Esther and should have been for Mrs. Hull. In those moments when we have unique opportunities to stand up for Jewish causes, for Jewish people and Jewish values, do we take advantage of those moments? Do we wonder, if even for a brief moment, whether being in the "right place at the right time" brings with it unique responsibilities? Esther was fortunate to have Mordecai to remind her. Mrs. Hull, unfortunately, did not have Mordecai, though in the scenario we described, a *non-Jewish* woman succeeded in saving the Jewish refugees. Who will we be in our lives? Esther at the beginning? Esther at the end? Mrs. Hull?

Felix Frankfurter and Jan Karski

Let's look at another example of Jewish behavior during this period of our history. Jan Karski was a Polish Catholic who, in 1943, risked his life and volunteered to enter the Warsaw Ghetto and the extermination camp in Belzec in order to report to the rest of the world what was really taking place there. Upon "escaping" from those places, he travelled around the world in the hopes of convincing world governments that more had to be done to save the Jews.

One of the people with whom Karski shared the harrowing images of what was happening to Europe's Jewish community was Felix Frankfurter, a Jewish member of the United States Supreme Court, and a close personal friend of President Roosevelt. Although Karski had been checked and rechecked by western intelligence both in Europe and in the United States (and had been shown to be telling the truth), the Jewish Justice Frankfurter listened to his report and responded "I cannot believe you."[14] Even when pressed, Frankfurter refused to back down, and never advocated the intervention that Karski believed was so important. As we now know, the Roosevelt administration stood by without bombing the railroad tracks to the various death camps, allowing hundreds of thousands of Jews who could have been saved to go to their deaths.

Let's return to our central question. Why would a Jew like Justice Frankfurter "balance" his loyalty as a Jew and his desire to serve the American judicial system by refusing to believe

Karski and by refusing to advocate that FDR intervene on the behalf of Frankfurter's own people?! Dershowitz claims that "Frankfurter did not want to be regarded as one of those soft-hearted Jews who put Jewish lives before the American war effort. He did not want to endanger his valuable credibility with the president over an issue of Jewish sentimentality."[15] Hillel might have said that Frankfurter was too concerned that others might say he was overly concerned with the fear of וּכְשֶׁאֲנִי לְעַצְמִי, מַה אֲנִי, "if I am only for myself, who am I?"

Did Frankfurter forget about אִם אֵין אֲנִי לִי מִי לִי, "if I am not for myself . . .?" David Wyman, a historian who has studied American reactions to genocide during World War II, believes that the answer is "yes." He notes that "[a]lthough [Frankfurter] used his contacts to press numerous policies and plans, rescue [of the Jews] was not among them."[16] In a more recent book, Jerold Auerbach insists that Frankfurter was representative of a broader class of Jews. "[N]othing was more characteristic of American Jews . . . than their acquiescence in Roosevelt's 'abandonment of the Jews' of Europe. Proximity to power . . . all but silenced them to Jewish tragedy."[17] What would Hillel have said had he seen this behavior? What about the author of the passage from the Sifrei? How do *we* feel less than fifty years later?

Eddie Jacobson and President Harry Truman

Happily, our chapter includes at least one narrative with a very different mode of behavior. In 1948, as each of the world's major powers was deciding how to respond to the pressure for the creation of a Jewish state, a little known Jewish clothing salesman played a crucial role for the Jewish people. Eddie Jacobson had been President Harry Truman's business partner in a men's clothing store before Truman's rise to power. Truman at the time, had been refusing to meet with anyone whom he felt might pressure him to act in one way or another on this issue. Merle Miller, Truman's biographer, recounts the following story:[18]

> And then late on the morning of March 13 Mr. Truman got a telephone call from the Statler, where his old friend and business partner Eddie Jacobson was staying. Eddie wanted to come to the White House to see the President.

> "I said to him, 'Eddie, I'm always glad to see old friends, but there's one thing you've got to promise me. I don't want you to say a word about what's going on over there in the Middle East. Do you promise?' And he did."

A little later Eddie was ushered into the Oval Room, and this is the way Harry Truman described what followed:

"Great tears were running down his cheeks, and I took one look at him, and I said, 'Eddie, you son of a b----, you promised me you wouldn't say a word about what's going on over there.' And he said, 'Mr. President, I haven't said a word, but every time I think of the homeless Jews, homeless for thousands of years, and I think about Dr. Weizmann [Chaim Weizmann, head of the World Zionists and the first President of Israel], I start crying. I can't help it. He's an old man, and he's spent his whole life working for a homeland for the Jews, and now he's sick, and he's in New York and wants to see you. And every time I think about it I can't help crying.'

"I said, 'Eddie, that's enough. That's the last word.'

"And so we talked about this and that, but every once in a while a big tear would roll down his cheek. At one point he said something about how I felt about old Andy Jackson, and he was crying again. He said he knew he wasn't supposed to but that's how he felt about Weizmann.

"I said, 'Eddie, you son of a b----, I ought to have you thrown right out of here from breaking your promise; you knew damn good and well I couldn't stand seeing you cry.'

"And he kind of smiled at me, still crying, though, and he said, 'Thank you, Mr. President,' and he left.

"After he was gone, I picked up the phone and called the State Department, and I told them I was going to see Weizmann. Well, you should have heard the carrying-on. The first thing they said - they said Israel wasn't even a country yet and didn't have a flag or anything. They said if Weizmann comes to the White House, what are we going to use for a flag?

"And I said, 'Look here; he's staying at the Waldorf-Astoria hotel in New York, and every time some foreign dignitary is staying there, they put something out. You find out what it is, and we'll use it. And I want you to call me right back.'"

On March 18 Chaim Weizmann came to the White House, but no flag was necessary. He came in through the east gate, and the fact of his visit was not known until later.

In any case, only eleven minutes after Israel became a state in May, its existence was officially recognized by the United States. . . A year later the Chief Rabbi of Israel came to see the President, and he told him, "God put you in your mother's womb so that you could be the instrument to bring about the rebirth of Israel after two thousand years."

At that, great tears started rolling down Harry Truman's cheeks.

Why did Harry Truman begin to cry at that moment? Did he realize that he'd been lucky enough to have a friend with the courage to push him to take the right action? Was he, perhaps, still shaken by the realization that without a phone call from his old friend Eddie Jacobson, history might have been very different? And what about Eddie Jacobson? What was it about this man that prevented him from being overwhelmed by the office of the President of the United States? Why did *he*, so powerless in comparison to Mrs. Hull and Justice Frankfurter, not relent? What does this story suggest about who really has power?

Thousands of years ago, Hillel provided us with an important maxim, seeking to balance our self-interest with our responsibility to work for the welfare of the larger society in which we live. At times, we've seen, that balance seems to have been out of kilter. We have seen what can happen when Jews like Mrs. Hull and Justice Frankfurter worry *too* much about כְּשֶׁאֲנִי לְעַצְמִי, מה אֲנִי. At times, it takes the actions of a simple but courageous man like Eddie Jacobson to remind us that in a non-Jewish world, Hillel's first claim may be the more important of the two we've discussed. At times, Eddie Jacobson might say to us today, living in a non-Jewish society makes it all the more important that we never forget how important it is that we remember אִם אֵין אֲנִי לִי מִי לִי, or if we are not for ourselves, no one will be for us.

Is there some Eddie Jacobson in each of us? How will we live to express it?

Questions for Discussion

1. Can you think of any instance in which you recall rising to the occasion and standing up for Jewish interests? How did that feel? Was it difficult? Why? Did it change your feelings about being Jewish? Why? How?

2. Aside from Mrs. Hulls's apparent decision not to interfere in her husband's professional affairs, what else can you surmise about her Jewish commitment from the little you know about her? How strongly did she feel part of her people? Which of her actions might have been different had she been committed to the Jewish people?

3. Why do you think Secretary of State Hull refused to admit the Jewish refugees to the United States? What might have been his concerns? Can you think of recent events in your own country or in other countries in which these concerns were an issue? Does thinking about *this* incident impact your views of those other situations? How? Why?

6. Are Jews in danger in parts of the world today? How can we help them? What things have you done to help Jews in other parts of the world? To lobby for Israel?

Activities

1. It is dinner time in the Hull residence. Select one person to play the role of Mrs. Hull, and another to be Secretary Hull. What is the nature of the conversation? Add three (fictitious) teenage children to the table. What do the children want to know? What do they ask their mother? What does she say? . . . . What do *you* learn from this "conversation?"

2. If you were Felix Frankfurther, would you have gone to President Roosevelt in order to ask him to intercede on behalf of the Jews? Select someone to play the role of Justice Frankfurter, and someone else to play another friend or family member of his. How does the conversation progress?

CHAPTER NINE
ישנו עם אחד
JEWISH DISTINCTIVENESS AND ANTI-SEMITISM

Throughout this Sourcebook, we have been stressing the importance of Jewish uniqueness and the need for a distinctive Jewish way of life if we are to live up to the challenge of serving as God's עַם סְגֻלָּה and an אוֹר לַגּוֹיִם. But as we have seen, it is much simpler to acknowledge that we are *supposed* to lead this sort of life than to actually do so. In the previous chapter, we looked at examples of three Jewish figures who sought to avoid playing the high profile roles they might have played because they feared that they might risk the positions which they had achieved.

For most of us, risking some high governmental position or other prominent post is not a consideration in our daily lives. But even though we are, for the most part, much more ordinary people than the figures we discussed in the previous chapter, we can understand their feelings. Many of us have experienced the feeling of being "too obviously" Jewish in a distinctly non-Jewish society, and know that such feelings are not at all comfortable. Indeed, at times we suspect that what is at stake is more than simply feeling uncomfortable. Rather, we suspect that should we continuously live and behave in a uniquely Jewish fashion, we will arouse more resentment against our community than we might if we just "lay low." [☞] Being "too Jewish," some Jews sometimes feel, might not be good for the Jews. As we'll now see, we are not the first generation of Jews to feel this way. The link between Jewish uniqueness and anti-semitism is an age-old issue.

Esther, Haman and Jewish Uniqueness

We have already discussed the story of Purim and Queen Esther's initial desire to avoid playing a risky role in saving the Jews of Shushan. Let's return to that story once again, for as we will see, the Book of Esther is in many respects a profound discussion of this very issue.

We have been taught from an early age to see Mordecai and Esther as great Jewish heroes. And for their eventual role in saving the Jews of Shushan, there is no doubt that they merit this reputation. But when we look carefully at the Book of Esther, we also see that the theme of Mordecai's and Esther's assimilation into Persian society lies just below the surface of the story.

Names, as we know, are an important way of stating who we are and what we believe is important. Many North American Jews today give their children distinctly Hebrew or Israeli names for that very reason, while others seek to avoid names that seem overly "non-Jewish." Even our tradition understands that names are important. The midrash suggests that the Children of Israel survived their years of slavery in Egypt as a distinctly Jewish nation because, among other reasons, they did not take on Egyptian names during that period. Whether that was true or not in ancient Egypt is a complicated issue; what is certain, however, is that it was *not* true of Mordecai and Esther. Biblical scholars tell us that Mordecai and Esther were distinctly *Persian* names. Indeed, these names were not only not Jewish, they were names taken from Babylonian gods. Mordecai is taken from the name of the Babylonian god "Marduk," while Esther comes from the name of the goddess "Ishtar."[19]

In addition to the issue of their names, there are other indications that Mordecai and Esther sought to hide their Jewishness so as to avoid anti-semitism. After all, what is Esther doing "marrying" the Persian king in the first place?! Had her Jewishness been something she intended to live proudly and openly, could she contemplate living in the King's harem? Indeed, the Megillah tells us specifically that Esther tries not to reveal to anyone that she was Jewish. Note what the Megillah tells us about Mordecai's instructions to Esther: (Est. 2:10) לֹא הִגִּידָה אֶסְתֵּר אֶת עַמָּהּ וְאֶת מוֹלַדְתָּהּ, כִּי מָרְדֳּכַי צִוָּה עָלֶיהָ אֲשֶׁר לֹא תַגִּיד, or "Esther did not reveal [the identity of] her people or her birth, for Mordecai had commanded her not to say [anything]." Esther and Mordecai, therefore, are committed to not revealing who they are, for they do not want to face the consequences that many of us also often fear.

But as we know, the "ruse" does not work. Something happens to Mordecai that makes him unable to conceal his identity. He can mask his identity only until he is confronted by the troublesome command to bow to Haman. Then he knows that he must confront who he is. The Megillah tells us that (Est. 3:1-5):

> After these things, King Ahasuerus promoted Haman the son of Hammedata the Agagite, and advanced him, and set his seat above all the princes who were with him. And all the king's servants who were in the king's gate bowed, and

honored Haman: for that is what the King had commanded. But Mordecai did not bow or honor him.

Mordecai's public demonstration of his Jewishness and his refusal to bow to Haman, however, infuriate Haman. And in a now classic passage, Haman ventures to the King and urges him to take extraordinary action. He says (Est. 3:8-9): יֶשְׁנוֹ עַם אֶחָד מְפֻזָּר וּמְפֹרָד בֵּין הָעַמִּים בְּכֹל מְדִינוֹת מַלְכוּתֶךָ, וְדָתֵיהֶם שֹׁנוֹת מִכָּל עָם וְאֶת דָּתֵי הַמֶּלֶךְ אֵינָם עֹשִׂים, וְלַמֶּלֶךְ אֵין שֹׁוֶה לְהַנִּיחָם. אִם עַל הַמֶּלֶךְ טוֹב יִכָּתֵב לְאַבְּדָם....; "there is a certain people scattered and dispersed among all the nations of your kingdom, and their laws are different from the laws of all [the other] peoples, and they do not obey the law of the king. It is not in the king's interest to allow them to endure ..."

Despite Mordecai's and Esther's attempt to conceal their Jewishness, their religious convictions do come to the fore. And as soon as Haman realizes that they are different from other people, he suggests to the king that these differences alone are reason enough not to allow them to survive. Simply being different, the Megillah reminds us, *can* sometimes arouse the worst possible reactions in people.

Tacitus Observes the Jews

Anti-semitism is not only a saddening and sometimes frightening phenomenon; it is also very complex. Not all forms of anti-semitism stem from the same sources, and not all derive from our uniquely Jewish patterns of behavior. But many do. Haman was surely not the only person in antiquity to make his argument. Listen to the words of Tacitus, an early Roman historian of the late first century:[20]

> To establish his influence over this people for all time, Moses introduced new religious practices, quite opposed to those of all other religions. The Jews regard as profane all that we hold sacred; on the other hand, they permit all that we abhor. . . . The other customs of the Jews are base and abominable . . . . [They are] the worst rascals among other peoples, [and always send] tribute and contributions to Jerusalem, thereby increasing the wealth of the Jews. [Again], the Jews are extremely loyal to one another, and always ready to show compassion, but toward every other people they feel only hate and enmity. They sit apart at meals . . . and abstain from intercourse with foreign women. They adopted circumcision to distinguish themselves from other peoples by this difference.

Although Tacitus' description of the Jews goes on for many more pages, this passage is certainly enough to enable us to see how he reacts to the Jews' "uniqueness." Note that at least *some* of what he says is not factually untrue. Jews, obviously concerned with the kinds of food they ate, probably *did* sit apart at meals. And as we would expect, Jewish men *did* avoid relationships with non-Jewish women. And while the purpose of *berit milah*, or circumcision, is not specifically for the purpose that Jewish men should appear different than non-Jewish men, in the ancient world that was obviously one of the results. But despite the "correctness" of some of his observations, Tacitus gives them a dangerous and disturbing slant. He reads the worst possible motivations into the Jewish traditions of which he is aware. Are we ourselves not also worried that our own contemporaries will do this? [☞]

So far, we have seen the relationship between Jewish uniqueness and anti-Jewish sentiment in the story of Haman and in Tacitus, both from the ancient world. Let's continue this exploration into the modern world, and see an example of how one extremely traditional European rabbi felt we ought to respond.

Jewish Service in the German Army

In the early part of this century, during the last generation of German Jewry prior to the Sho'ah, one of the greatest halakhic authorities was a man named Rabbi David Zevi Hoffmann. Like many halakhic authorities of our own time, he responded to hundreds of Jewish legal questions submitted to him from far and wide. When another rabbi felt incapable of answering a difficult question, he would submit it to someone like Rabbi Hoffmann. Hoffmann's answers to these questions are called responsa (the singular is responsum); the Hebrew terminology for this important literature is שְׁאֵלוֹת וּתְשׁוּבוֹת, which literally means "questions and answers."

On one occasion, Rabbi Hoffmann was asked a fascinating question.[21] The rabbi submitting the question explained that a young Jewish man had just been ordered to report for service in the German army. This young man, an observant Jew, was unsure what to do. On the one hand, the law was clear; he was required to report for army service. On the other hand, however, he knew that serving in the Germany army would obligate him to violate Jewish law pertaining to Shabbat and the Festivals, and probably kashrut as well. His question, therefore, was whether to flee the draft and to maintain his high level of observance, or to report for military duty in full knowledge of the fact that his observance would have to be curtailed.

Hoffmann's response, which is complex, concludes with a fascinating logic:

> Behold there is no doubt that [the position] that he not evade the army . . . is more than a commandment, for anyone who does so causes a desecration of God's name, if the matter should become known and cause harm to the Jews. For the haters of the Jews claim that the Jews do not perform the laws of the State.

Hoffmann then continues several lines later and adds:

> it is a logical conclusion that if he does not go of his own accord, but rather is taken by the law of the State, he does not have to flee even though he will have to violate the Shabbat, since by fleeing he may cause more obstacles [for Jews in Germany]. Therefore, the principle of "sit and do not act" is definitely preferable to [the fulfillment of] a commandment.

> Moreover, if we shall say that he is obligated to flee so that he should not be obliged to violate the Shabbat, all Jewish men will feel so compelled, and most will not succeed [in fleeing] and this will cause a great desecration of God's name, Heaven forbid, for naught. It is therefore best that you observe the command of the King, and perhaps you will find favor in the eyes of your officers, and they will permit you to observe the Shabbat, and you will [succeed in] doing good for both God and man. . . And if you perform all your actions for the sake of Heaven, all will be at peace with you, and you can abide in the land and remain loyal and peace [will descend] on Israel.

In what may strike us as a very surprising ruling, Rabbi Hoffmann — effectively the head of the German Orthodox community at that time — rules that Jews need to "lie low," even at the expense of violating some of the commandments. And the language he uses is worth noting. When he says non-Jews will accuse Jews of not obeying the law of the state, he uses the phrase אֵינָם עוֹשִׂים אֶת דָּתֵי הַמַּלְכוּת (they do not obey the laws of the kingdom), which is only a slight paraphrase of Esther 3:8, which we said above reads וְאֶת דָּתֵי הַמֶּלֶךְ אֵינָם עֹשִׂים translated as "who do not obey the King's laws." This language is not accidental. Hoffmann, who lives in a period when German Jews are just beginning to make headway into German professional and social life, does not want to risk that progress. He reminds his readers that this issue is a perennial one for Jews, and that as far back as Haman, Jews have encountered danger by being perceived as different and, as a result, not committed to the interests of the rest of society. German Jews, Hoffmann believes, ought to work hard to avoid having that said about them, even at rather great cost.

But Does It Work? And Does It Need To?

But is the pattern that Rabbi Hoffmann suggests still applicable to our world? We need to recall that scarcely one generation after Rabbi Hoffmann wrote those words, most of German Jewry had been murdered by the Nazis, even though the vast majority of German Jews had assimilated to unprecedented degrees. And Mordecai and Esther, though they had adopted Persian names and lifestyles, also found themselves in danger. How, then, should *we* react? Is our world in any way similar to that of Mordecai and Esther or Rabbi Hoffmann's early twentieth century German Jewish community? At least one person thinks matters today are very different, and that we ought to begin to recognize that.

Alan Dershowitz, whose book *Chutzpah* we also discussed in the previous chapter, states in his introduction:[22]

> . . . a century after the arrival of Jews in significant numbers to America's shores, the time has come for us to shed our self-imposed second-class status, drop our defensiveness, and rid ourselves of our pathological fear of offending our "hosts." We must strike from our vocabulary the offensive concept of *shanda fur de goyim* — an embarrassment in front of the gentiles. . . .

Rather, Dershowitz continues:

> The byword of past generations of Jewish Americans has been *shanda*— fear of embarrassment in front of our hosts. The byword of the next generation should be *chutzpah* — assertive insistence on first-class status among our peers.

While Professor Dershowitz' advice for modern North American Jews sounds exciting and ideal, do we feel as secure in our home cities, our non-Jewish schools and our non-Jewish neighborhoods as he suggests we should? [☞] Why, or why not? And if we do not feel secure, what ought we do? Should we seek to hide our Jewishness? Will that ultimately work? Can we live the mandate of being an עַם סְגֻלָּה and an אוֹר לַגּוֹיִם if we live our Jewishness privately? Is it possible that Professor Dershowitz is partly right and partly wrong; is it possible that the risks *might* still exist, but that the costs of not living our Judaism openly and proudly are still too great? Why, ultimately, are we Jewish? And how do we need to live to reflect that?

Questions for Discussion

1. How would you feel about the idea of wearing a kippah in public? How about ẓiẓit? Why do you think that even very committed USY'ers sometimes hesitate to wear these ritual objects? Are your peers concerned about appearing "too Jewish?" Are you?

2. How do you feel about Professor Dershowitz' comments as they were quoted in this Chapter? Do you agree? Disagree? Why?

3. Have you every had experiences — such as those suggested in Tacitus — when someone saw a Jewish custom, observance or practice, and assumed that it had some negative motivation that actually had nothing to do with the actual reason for the custom? What was the situation? Did you say anything? Why? What did you say? How did you feel at that moment?

Activities

1. You and your "spouse" are expecting a child in two months. The time has come to decide on names. What kinds of names do you think a Jewish child living in North America should have? Select a "spouse" who has a different point of view. What issues get raised in your conversation?

2. You have just learned that during the previous night, someone painted a swastika on the wall of your synagogue. Your USY Chapter is now meeting, discussing what you should do in response. What are the possibilities? What are the advantages and disadvantages of each? What will you decide to recommend to the rabbi? What can *you* do?

3. You have just learned that Leonard Jeffries, a very anti-semitic African-American leader, is coming to speak at your High School on an unknown topic. Some non-Jewish students

are thrilled, but others are opposed, and plan to protest. Should Jews join the protest? Should they make it clear they are protesting because they are Jewish? Would our answer differ if other non-Jewish students were not already planning to demonstrate? You are sitting at a table with a group of Jewish leaders in your school. How does the conversation unfold?

CHAPTER TEN
והביאותים אל אדמתם
JEWISH LIFE IN A JEWISH HOMELAND

Throughout this Sourcebook, we have been examining the complexity of Jewish life in the diaspora. Our survey of Jewish uniqueness has taken us from the concepts of "chosen people" and "holy people" to questions of balancing our responsibilities to those around us with our obligations to our own community, and most recently, to the sometimes unpleasant ramifications of living as a people always different from those around us. There is a paradox worth noting here: if we are to live up to our awesome responsibilities as God's "treasured nation," we need to live lives which are sometimes very different from the lives of our non-Jewish neighbors.

In many ways, then, this Sourcebook has addressed themes surrounding the issue of "living as a Jew in a non-Jewish world." We have seen that the challenge of Jewish life in a non-Jewish world is not a simple one. If we choose not to live lives that are different in some important respects, then it seems we will have to give up a piece of what it means to be a Jew in the full sense of what we now know that means. This sounds difficult, and it is. Is there no alternative? Is there any place in the world in which we can escape this dilemma? That, too, is a complicated question, and in the following pages, we will examine some classic Jewish sources and prominent Jewish thinkers who have addressed that problem.

Biblical Sources and the Jewish Homeland

For many of us, life as Jews in North America seems natural. We have become used to being the "other" in a non-Jewish society, and have learned to cope with the challenges of diaspora Jewish life reasonably well. But as comfortable as we may feel, the Torah has a very different conception than we do of how — and where — Jews should live their lives.

Some of the Torah's most important lessons about the importance of a Jewish homeland emerge from the stories we are taught about the very beginnings of God's relationship with the Jewish people. We learn a great deal from the first words that God speaks to the first Jew. When God first speaks to Abram, God's concern is not with Abram's beliefs or observances, but with where Abram will live. At the start of Genesis 12, the Torah records the following pivotal words in Jewish history: וַיֹּאמֶר ה' אֶל אַבְרָם: לֶךְ לְךָ מֵאַרְצְךָ וּמִמּוֹלַדְתְּךָ וּמִבֵּית אָבִיךָ אֶל-הָאָרֶץ אֲשֶׁר אַרְאֶךָּ; "The Lord said to Abram, 'Go forth from your native land and from your father's house to the land that I will show you." Thus, God's very first words to the Jewish people teach that the Jews belong in a certain place — the place we now call Israel.

Later, when God decides to liberate the Children of Israel from Egyptian slavery, God commands Moses to lead them not only out of Egypt, but to the Promised Land. As the Jewish people begins its forty year odyssey towards the "land of milk and honey," God seems to suggest that a fulfilled Jewish national life must unfold in a uniquely Jewish place. Thus, Moses spends almost his entire life leading his people to that place; the vast majority of the Torah, in fact, focuses on the Jewish people not just as they wander through the desert, but as the march steadily towards the Promised Land, and toward their destiny.

Later in the Bible, the prophet Ezekiel makes this point most clearly. Ezekiel foresees a solution to the difficulties Jews experience throughout the world, and in Chapter 34, he uses the beautiful and common image of the shepherd to describe how God will care for Israel. Beginning with the middle of verse 11, God exclaims: הִנְנִי אָנִי וְדָרַשְׁתִּי אֶת צֹאנִי וּבִקַּרְתִּים. כְּבַקָּרַת רֹעֶה עֶדְרוֹ בְּיוֹם הֱיוֹתוֹ בְתוֹךְ צֹאנוֹ נִפְרָשׁוֹת כֵּן אֲבַקֵּר אֶת צֹאנִי, וְהִצַּלְתִּי אֶתְהֶם מִכָּל הַמְּקוֹמֹת אֲשֶׁר נָפֹצוּ שָׁם בְּיוֹם עָנָן וַעֲרָפֶל. וְהוֹצֵאתִים מִן הָעַמִּים וְקִבַּצְתִּים מִן הָאֲרָצוֹת וַהֲבִיאוֹתִים אֶל אַדְמָתָם; "I am going to search out My flock, and I will seek them out. As a shepherd seeks out his flock when some of them have become detached [from the rest], so I will seek out My flock; I will rescue them from the places to which they were scattered on the [sad] day of cloud and fog. I will remove them from among the other nations, gather them together from the lands, and I will bring them to their land."

How does God plan to rescue and revive the Jewish people in this passage? The plan is simple; God will bring them together from all the places on the earth to which they have been scattered, and they will live a new and fulfilled life in a land which is uniquely theirs. Jewish life is most intense and nurturing, this passage from Ezekiel suggests, when it is *not* lived among the nations; rather, the Tanakh suggests in this passage, ideal Jewish life might be life lived completely on our own terms, in our own place and exclusively among our own people.

But is the Bible the only place in which our people has expressed its yearning for a place of our own, for a "stage" on which the drama of our national history could unfold? Certainly not! As we'll now see, our prayerbook also expresses this hope, reminding us daily of the centrality a Jewish homeland has always had in Jewish consciousness.

The "Promised Land" in Jewish Prayer

The *siddur*, the collection of prayers that traditional Jews encounter each and every day, reminds us time and again of the importance of a Jewish homeland for a richly lived Jewish life. As Jews prepare to recite the *Shema*, one of the most intensive moments of the morning service, we utter the following passionate plea: וַהֲבִיאֵנוּ לְשָׁלוֹם מֵאַרְבַּע כַּנְפוֹת הָאָרֶץ וְתוֹלִיכֵנוּ קוֹמְמִיּוּת לְאַרְצֵנוּ; "Gather us in peace from the four corners of the earth, and lead us in dignity to our land." What is it that we think of immediately prior to reciting "Hear O Israel?" We think of a homeland of our own, and plead with God to make that possible. And how do we position our bodies during the entire service? We face Jerusalem, expressing our sense that our prayers for renewed and perfected Jewish life might well be fulfilled more quickly in our own land.

Similarly, as we begin *Birkat Ha-Mazon* (the Blessing after Meals) on Shabbat and Holidays, we recite the passage called *Shir Ha-Ma'alot*, taken from Psalm 126. How does that Psalm begin? We begin our praise of God and our song by reciting: שִׁיר הַמַּעֲלוֹת. בְּשׁוּב ה' אֶת שִׁיבַת צִיּוֹן הָיִינוּ כְּחֹלְמִים. אָז יִמָּלֵא שְׂחוֹק פִּינוּ, וּלְשׁוֹנֵנוּ רִנָּה. "A song of ascents. When the Lord brought back those that returned to Zion — we were like dreamers — our mouths shall be filled with laughter, our tongues, with songs of joy." What do we say will make us happiest as a people? What would make our gladness complete? God's restoring the fortunes of Zion, God's rebuilding the Jewish nation in the Jewish homeland. Even as we prepare to thank God for the sustenance our food has provided us, we remind ourselves that true Jewish flourishing will require more than food. It will require a place in which we can live our collective national dream. True Jewish flourishing, the *Shir Ha-ma'alot* reminds us, requires a homeland.

Even our joy at the Passover Seder, the moment in which we celebrate our freedom from Egyptian slavery and other forms of bondage, is not complete without the idea of Jewish people returning to their homeland. For each year, as we conclude the Seder, we shift our attention away from Egypt as we recite the phrase לְשָׁנָה הַבָּאָה בִּירוּשָׁלָיִם, "next year in Jerusalem." Although we are free, we remind ourselves, we have still not fulfilled the ultimate Jewish dream. For the *real* Jewish dream is not just freedom from other peoples' tyranny, but a freedom in which we can express the full meaning and richness of Jewish life. That richness, the Passover *Haggadah* reminds us, will only receive *full* expression in a uniquely *Jewish* homeland.

Is the dream still alive? Do modern Jews still believe that Israel and Jewish life in the Jewish state offer us something that no other form of Jewish life can? As we will see, the dream is very much alive, but different Jews visualize the dream in dissimilar ways. Let's look at a few expressions of this dream for a Jewish state. As we do, we'll see at least three very different conceptions of what a Jewish state should be.

Letters to an American Jewish Friend

Hillel Halkin's *Letters to an American Jewish Friend* is one of the best known Zionist compositions of our time. In these "letters," the author (who has moved to Israel) writes a friend still in America and seeks to convey his passion for life in Israel. The following passage, taken from that book, seems to echo Ezekiel's hopes some twenty-five hundred years later:[23]

> If we in Israel succeed, the long march that began nearly a century ago in Europe will be over. We will be home again. We will become like the Gentiles, an ordinary people with an ordinary culture of its own, which is like, in the words of the Psalm, "a tree planted by streams of water that yields its fruit in season and its leaf does not wither." On that day there will be no need to ask anymore who is a Jew and who is an Israeli, or what is the difference between them, because the two words will have come to mean a single thing. [☞]

On one level, it would be hard to quibble with this vision. After all, who would not long to see a world in which Jews did not experience the feelings of discomfort at being "out of place" that we've spoken of throughout these chapters? Have we not all sometimes yearned for lives which were not complicated by the realities of living as Jews in a non-Jewish world? Many of us have had the experience of wishing for exactly that, and on that level, Halkin's dream makes perfect sense, even if we may not believe it is likely to come to fruition in the near future.

But think about Halkin's dream some more, this time in light of everything we've studied together thus far. Which of the topics we've discussed would still be meaningful in a completely Jewish society? Could we be an עַם סְגֻלָּה? How about an עַם קָדוֹשׁ? Would we have to give up on the ideal of being an אוֹר לַגּוֹיִם? How would we maintain the relevance of all the concepts we've studied in these chapters? *Could* we? If we concluded that we had to give them up, could we still maintain the "soul" of our Jewishness? Does that even matter?

Surprising as it might seem, some passionate Zionists do not believe that the State of Israel needs to be a place where some unqiue "soul" of Jewisnness can survive. These people suggest that what should be Jewish about the Jewish state is only its people, not its underlying philosophy. Consider the words of Amnon Rubinstein, a member of the Israeli Knesset from the "Meretz" party:

> "The State of Israel" is, at times, defined as a Jewish State. But this definition misses the mark. A State cannot be Jewish since it is not a creation of Judaism. From a religious viewpoint, a Jewish State implies a halakhic state, one in which the Mosaic Torah is the only code of law, whereas from a free, liberal non-halakhic point of view, there is difficulty in attaching the term "Jew" to a State which is entirely a social and state instrument. It would be preferable, in my view, to return to Herzl's original definition: Israel is the State of the Jews. [☞]

Can the Jewish State really not be Jewish? Would we be satisfied with a Jewish State that was Jewish solely because Jewish people lived there? Is *that* why God wanted Abram to go to "the land that I will show you?" Is *that* what the Jewish people wandered forty years in the desert to reach? Is *that* what we pray for each and every day?

There are no easy answers to these questions. For even if we claim that we want something more for the Jewish State than the fact that it be the State of the Jews, *what exactly* do we want?! *How* should the Jewish State be Jewish? What shall we do about those citizens of the State who are not Jewish, or who are Jewish but do not share the majority's conception of what Judaism stands for? Can Israel have a particular Jewish agenda and still respect the individuality and the rights of these varied people?

Some people believe that as difficult as that challenge might be, Israel's soul — and not only her citizens — needs to be Jewish. Rabbi I. Amital, the Rosh Yeshivah of the Gush

Etziyon Yeshivah (one of Israel's prestigious academies of traditional learning), seems to disagree with Rubenstein, as he writes the following:

> Another form of Zionism also exists, the Zionism of redemption. This Zionism did not emerge in order to solve the Jewish Question through the establishment of a Jewish State, but to serve as the Lord's vehicle for preparing Israel for its redemption. Its internal objective is not the normalization of the Jewish Nation to be a nation like all nations, but to be a holy people, the nation of a Living God, whose center will be Jerusalem, sanctified by the presence of God's Temple.

For Rabbi Amital, the dream of a Jewish State is a dream of giving life to the very *uniqueness* of the Jewish people. He wants no part of a dream in which Israel becomes a state much like other states. For him, to deserve to be called the *Jewish* state, Israel has to become the modern incarnation of the ancient biblical ideal that Jews serve as a "treasured" and "holy" people.

Jewish Life in a Jewish Homeland?

So where should Jewish life ideally be lived? Is it possible that only outside of Israel — where we are surrounded by non-Jewish cultures — Jews will recall their unique mission? Our tradition seems to reject that idea. Or does our tradition side with Hillel Halkin, who argues that the goal is to become a nation like all others, living in our own land? But then what about our unique role in the world? Or should we seek to fulfill the dream of a unique Israel which serves as a light unto the nations? But how does that *really* happen? Doesn't modern Israeli experience seem to teach us that all modern states, no matter how idealistic, have to make terribly difficult decisions about the use of force, the treatment of their citizens and basic issues of security and survival? Could a "holy" or "treasured" people survive in that competitive and often cruel arena?

These are profoundly difficult questions, but that is what is so exciting about the modern State of Israel. Israel is the place in which Jews once again participate as important decision-makers on the world's stage. Thus, Israel offers Jews the opportunity and the responsibility to reflect Jewish values in the midst of life's most agonizing questions. No longer are Jewish values and Jewish dreams for humanity merely intellectual pursuits discussed in the academies of learning. Now, with a safe, secure and strong Jewish state, we have the chance to see if we can actually take our dreams for the world and make them reality.

Isn't that why many North American youth, perhaps you among them, have felt themselves come alive Jewishly in Israel like never before? How can we describe the feeling of preparing for Shabbat in Jerusalem, as virtually an entire city begins to slow down, flower vendors appear throughout downtown and a peace unlike any other begins to descend? Perhaps we see ourselves not as "the other" but as proud and authentic participants in world affairs when we walk down the same streets which King David walked, where the Maccabees struggled to maintain their religious identity and which Rabbi Akiva also knew?

All of us, according to Israeli law, have the option of becoming Israeli citizens. All we have to do is go. And certainly, most of us can find an opportunity to visit and to taste Israeli life, sampling perhaps for the first time what it is to really belong. When we feel the power and the passion of that experience, we sometimes feel ourselves profoundly changed. At the very least, we then need to ask ourselves some very important questions. What is it about Israel that enables us to come so alive as Jews? Are we still committed to our mission? If so, where and how ought we live to make ourselves God's עַם סְגֻלָּה?

Questions for Discussion

1. For almost two thousand years, Jews throughout the world dreamt of the possibility of returning to their homeland. Ironically, now that we have that chance, most Jews have elected not to go. Why do you think that is? Would *you* consider moving to Israel? Why? When?

2. What do *you* think a Jewish state should really be? Think of some of the greatest challenges currently facing the State of Israel. Do you believe that Israel — because it is a Jewish state — should address those challenges differently than other countries would? Try to give some specific examples of how you think that should happen.

3. In light of this Sourcebook, define "Jew." What is a Jew?

Activities

You are asked to play a role in a debate on the following question: "Is it possible to be Jewish in a non-Jewish world?" Which position do you choose to defend? Select someone to play the opposite role. Have the debate.

What are the major issues that get raised in this discussion? Do you learn something new from having to defend your position? Do you learn something from hearing the other person's position? What do you believe in your heart of hearts?

ENDNOTES

[Note: Endnotes refer to author and title only.
Complete bibliographic information may be found in the Works Cited section.]

1. Abraham Joshua Heschel, *God in Search of Man*, p. 425. Emphasis added.

2. Steven T. Katz, *Jewish Ideas and Concepts*, p. 139.

3. The following translation is a modified form of that found in *The Jerusalem Bible*. I have modified the language only for the purpose of making Paul's claim easier to comprehend.

4. David Novak, *Jewish-Christian Dialogue: A Jewish Justification*, p. 73.

5. Jacob Neusner, "The Jewish-Christian Argument in the First Century: Different People Talking about Different Things to Different People," p. 150.

6. Adolf von Harnack, *What is Christianity?*, pp. 122-123. Cited in Novak, p. 75.

7. Yosef Hayim Yerushalmi, *Freud's Moses: Judaism Terminable and Interminable*. This passage is also cited in David Stern's review of that volume, entitled "The Ego and the Yid," pp. 43-49.

8. Alberta Eiseman, *Rebels and Reformers*, p. 87.

9. The entire verse reads as following, according to the JPS translation: "If you lend money to My people, to the poor among you, do not act toward them as a creditor: exact no interest from them." Rav Yosef's statement quotes only the first part of the verse, and the translation of the rabbinic passage follows suit. We will have occasion to look at the entire verse just below.

10. Louis Finkelstein, ספרי על ספר דברים, Re'eh 15 (p. 175).

11. See the *Torah Temimah* on Deut. 22:24, comment 200 ('ר).

12. Alan Dershowitz, *Chutzpah*, p. 3.

13. This description is based on the account in Arthur D. Morse, *While Six Million Died: A Chronicle of American Apathy*, pp. 29-33.

14. This account is based upon Alan Dershowitz' *Chutzpah*, pp. 279 ff., David Wyman's *The Abandonment of the Jews*, pp. 314 ff. and Jerold Auerbach's *Rabbis and Lawyers*, pp. 162 ff. This particular citation is taken from Dershowitz, p. 281.

15. Dershowitz, pp. 281-282.

16. Wyman, p. 316, quoted again in Dershowitz, p. 282.

17. Auerbach, pp. 163-165, quoted again in Dershowitz, p. 282.

18. Merle Miller, *Plain Speaking*, pp. 217-218.

19. Moore, Carey A. *Esther: Introduction, Translation and Notes*, p. 19.

20. Tacitus, *The Histories*, Book V, pp. 179 ff. These quotations are selected from a very lengthy passage. In order to make the text as readable as possible, I have not adhered to strict stylistic rules regarding the use of ellipses. Thus, this passage should not be construed a precise quotation.

21. David Z. Hoffmann, *Melamed Le-Ho'il*, Vol. I, no. 42.

22. Dershowitz, pp. 7 and 9.

23. Hillel Halkin, *Letters to an American Jewish Friend*. Original page unkown; photocopy of text on file with author.

Works Cited

Auerbach, Jerold S. *Rabbis and Lawyers: The Journey from Torah to Constitution*. Bloomington: Indiana University Press, 1990.

Dershowitz, Alan. *Chutzpah*. Boston: Little, Brown and Company, 1991.

Eiseman, Alberta. *Rebels and Reformers*. Garden City: Zenith Books, 1976.

Epstein, Baruch Ha -Levi. *Torah Temimah*. New York: Keren Tora Publishing, 1904.

Finkelstein, Louis, ed. *Sifre on Deuteronomy*, New York: Jewish Theological Seminary of America, 1969.

Halkin, Hillel. *Letters to an American Jewish Friend*. Philadelphia: Jewish Publication Society, 1977.

Heschel, Abraham Joshua. *God in Search of Man*. Philadelphia: Jewish Publication Society of America, 1956.

Hoffmann, David Zevi. *Melamed Le-Ho'il*. Frankfort-am-Main: Herman Verlag, 1926.

Jones, Alexander, General Editor. *The Jerusalem Bible: Reader's Edition*, Garden City, NY: Doubleday & Company, Inc., 1966.

Katz, Steven T. *Jewish Ideas and Concepts*. Jerusalem: Keter Publishing House, Ltd., 1977.

Miller, Merle. *Plain Speaking: An Oral Biography of Harry S. Truman*. New York: G.P. Putnam's Sons, 1973.

Moore, Carey A. *Esther: Introduction, Translation and Notes*. Garden City, New York: Doubleday & Compnay, Inc., 1976.

Morse, Arthur D. *While Six Million Died: A Chronicle of American Apathy*. New York: Random House, 1967.

Neusner, Jacob. "The Jewish-Christian Argument in the First Century: Different People Talking about Different Things to Different People." *Crosscurrents* XXXV, no. 2-3 (June 1985).

Novak, David. *Jewish-Christian Dialogue: A Jewish Justification*. New York: Oxford University Press, 1989.

Stern, David. "The Ego and the Yid." *The New Republic* 207, no. 13 (21 September 1992): 43-49.

Tacitus. *The Histories*. Cambridge: Harvard University Press, 1931.

von Harnak, Adolph. *What Is Christianity?*, 2d rev. ed., trans. T.B. Saunders ed. New York and London: 1901.

Wyman, David S. *The Abandonment of the Jews: American and the Holocaust, 1941-1945*. New York: Pantheon Books, 1984.

Yerushalmi, Yosef Hayim. *Freud's Moses: Judaism Terminable and Interminable*. New Haven: Yale University Press, 1992.